KADH FORCE VIETNAM

KELLY, AGON, DILLARD & HARBAUGH

A Tale of Enterprise and Adventure in the Vietnam War

"There's a race of men that don't fit in,
A race that can't sit still;
So they break the hearts of kith and kin, And they roam the world at will.
They range the field and rove the flood,
And they climb the mountain's crest; Theirs is the curse of the gypsy blood,
And they don't know how to rest." **Robert Service**

AF473571

By Daniel Warvelle Harbaugh

KADH Force Vietnam

Danzmark Productions, Houston, Texas

TABLE OF CONTENTS

KADH FORMATION - A gathering of Eagles

In May 1966, by chance on a dock in the Saigon River, four adventurers met – Mike Kelly, Gary Dillard, Stu Agon - three ex-Army Special Forces troops; and Dan Harbaugh, USN WW II, now Captain of the US Navy contracted hydrographic survey vessel MS MARGA HENN , just arrived from Bangkok, Thailand. The six-man Thai crew had mutinied after the ship was caught in a night battle between a US Navy gunboat and the enemy onshore at the approach to Vung Tau; they demanded the ship turn around and go back to Bangkok.

The Thai crew looked like pirates and carried big knives on their belts, and were usually barefoot while onboard. For the next two days, Capt. Dan slept with tacks spread over his cabin floor to deter any barefoot mutineers; a procedure recalled from reading Joseph Conrad sea stories.

On the last night before docking at Saigon, Dan got an urgent 'nature's call', jumped out of his bunk onto his own tacks, followed by a loud yell. The Thai crew, expecting an enemy boarding party, came running, saw what had happened and all had a good laugh over it. After that relations were cordial, but the crew still wanted to return to Bangkok. Two of the crew, 'Pittoon', wheelsman, and 'Vittoon', engineer, were convinced to stay; the rest flown back to Bangkok.

KADH Force Vietnam

Short of a crew, the word was spread around the Saigon waterfront; Mike, Gary and Stu emerged on the dock out of a cloud of tear gas from a huge demonstration by the Buddhists and the police were attacking them with batons and tear gas. One Buddhist Monk knelt and immolated himself with burning gasoline; Mike, rather irreverently, referred to the Monk as a 'Buddha burger' and 'You want fries with that?'

Mike and Stu were immediately hired; Gary was working with RMK Marine Div. and joined later – the beginning of the 'KADH' Force.

Below: Kelly, Dillard, Harbaugh, Agon

KADH Executive Meeting in Saigon 1966.

OCEAN SCIENCE & ENGINEERING INC.

The US Navy OICC ,Officer-In-Charge-Construction, Vietnam hydrographic survey contract was awarded to 'Ocean Science & Engineering Inc.' of Washington DC, a group founded by Willard Newell Bascom, (1916-2000), noted engineer and oceanographer who pioneered deep-sea exploration. The OSE management staff in Saigon was a top-heavy absolutely incompetent 4-man cluster; including George Erlanger, Fred Libby, Dick O'Hagan, and Bob Miranda, a draftsman; all of whom were paper-shuffling desk-jockeys too chicken to venture out in a war zone. Erlanger, Libby and O'Hagan were all college graduates, ostensibly justified there to seek out new contract opportunities while accomplishing the current contract. They spent much time Hong Kong and Singapore and were useless in Vietnam.

One purpose of the hydrographic surveys was to map the sea bottom in major Vietnam seaports for dock construction and dredging shipping channels to enable large ships to dock; plus to show the dredge quantities in cubic meters for payment to the large contracted hydraulic dredges. Another purpose was to do soils coring at dock construction sites to determine the depth to drive pilings. Surveys were conducted in rivers to locate sand deposits for use in land filling and construction of river ports.

Dan was working on a Masters Degree at Long Beach State U.. He was acquainted with OSE from them chartering his boat MV NEREID for underwater mining tests. OSE wrote a letter to get Dan out of classes and enable return later.

CABLE ADDRESS: OCEANS TELEX: 089475 OCEANS WSH TELEPHONE: 301 - 657-4222

OCEAN SCIENCE AND ENGINEERING, INC.
OCEAN SCIENCE BUILDING
4905 DEL RAY AVENUE
WASHINGTON, D.C. 20014

May 2, 1966

Faculty Concerned
California State College at
Long Beach
Long Beach, California

Re: Withdrawal from classes by
Daniel W. Harbaugh

The services of Daniel W. Harbaugh, Oceanographic Specialist, are required immediately in the Viet Nam War Zone in the national interest.

Any provisions to enable Mr. Harbaugh to complete the semesters work in absentia, or at a later date, will be appreciated.

We will furnish further information on request.

Very truly yours,

E. E. Horton

Edward E. Horton

DH/sak

The KADH gang successfully accomplished numerous hydrographic surveys for OSE in the Saigon River and Mekong Delta, and then sailed up the China Sea coast to Cam Ranh Bay. Enroute they paused to 'thoroughly inspect' the Panamanian freighter 'EASTERN MARINER', after it hit a mine in the Saigon River near Nha Be. Suffice to say, the KADH boarding party 'liberated' everything on the ship that wasn't securely fastened, including 100's of China Sea and Indian Ocean nautical charts, the SSB & VHF radios and the radar; to, as Mike said, keep it out of the hands of the enemy. The ship was sunk on the enemy side of the river and there were a few 'booby traps' that demo-expert Mike disposed of.

Mike and Dan on the EASTERN MARINER. The noise of Mike exploding the bobby traps attracted a curious Navy patrol boat which came by and, noting the American flag on the skiff, shouted "You guys

working?" Up on the radar mast, Mike yelled: "Yeah, we're working!" The Navy guys returned, "OK, but be careful, the area is mined and 'Charlie' starts shooting around dusk!"

Part of the loot ...correction: 'liberated articles', from the EASTERN MARINER, after Mike blew the Captain's safe, was a stack of blank Panamanian seamen photo ID cards. By inserting KADH member's photo, a German name, and laminating the cards in clear plastic, the gang ignored the 10:00 PM curfew in effect for all American military and civilians in Saigon and major cities; a social detriment clearing out all the bars and night clubs just when things got interesting with the 'Tea Girls'. When challenged by the US Army Military Police patrols, they showed their seaman ID card and replied "Ich bin eine deutsche zeeman." The MPs would invariably say "Alright, alright ...you can stay."

"United States Naval Operations Vietnam, *Highlights*; May 1966

The PBRs reported that the ship EASTERN MARINER, of Panamanian registry and carrying a cargo of 4000 tons of bagged cement, was settling by the stern with a slight starboard list. Twelve feet of freeboard was remaining and the crew was abandoning ship. The PBRs and RAG 22 units rescued the crew and brought them to Nha Be., There were no casualties.

Divers revealed a twelve foot by ten foot hole in the starboard quarter and recovered remnants of nylon cord, indicating that a mine had been attached to the ship."

http://www.history.navy.mil/docs/vietnam/high66-5.html

On 20 Sept.,1966, OSE received orders from the Navy to do a hydrographic survey on Da Nang harbor at the North boundary of South Vietnam. Sailing the MARGA HENN from Cam Ranh Bay was impractical for this small project, so the survey crew and equipment were to be flown up by military transport aircraft. As usual, OSE wanted to load the expedition up with Saigon office experts. Dan sent the below radio message: “Harbaugh tired of running kindergarten for OSE experts”, and stated he would either go to Da Nang with Kelly, Agon and Dillard or “Advise or fire”; the KADH team went.

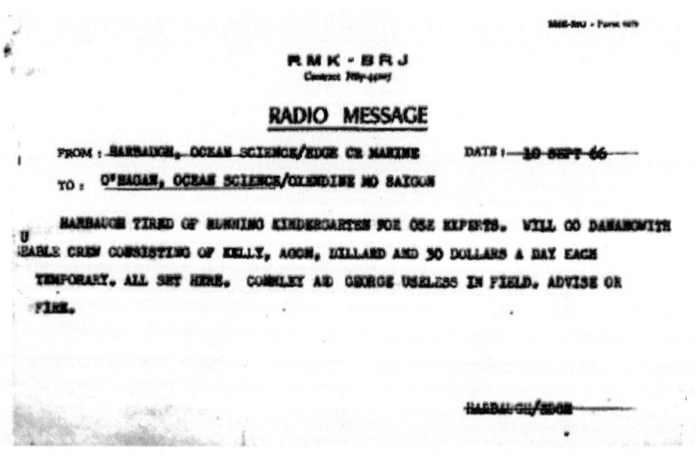

RMK - BRJ

RADIO MESSAGE

FROM : HARBAUGH, OCEAN SCIENCE/EDGE CR MARINE DATE : 20 SEPT 66

TO : O'HAGAN, OCEAN SCIENCE/OLENDINE MO SAIGON

HARBAUGH TIRED OF RUNNING KINDERGARTEN FOR OSE EXPERTS. WILL GO DANANGWITH UEABLE CREW CONSISTING OF KELLY, AGON, DILLARD AND 30 DOLLARS A DAY EACH TEMPORARY. ALL SET HERE. CONNLEY AND GEORGE USELESS IN FIELD. ADVISE OR FIRE.

HARBAUGH/EDGE

One of the dumb things OSE required the hydrographic survey crews to do was chop holes in the jungle and set range-lines for the survey boat to visually follow.

The survey boat steered by staying on the range-line and distances between radio fixes were determined by guessing at the speed of the boat.

In the subsequent US Navy/Exploration Science Inc. Navy contract, two onshore theodolites and intersecting angles were used to track and triangulate the boat radio fixes; no chopping required.

One of the OSE Saigon experts was 'Fat Bob' Miranda, a slob draftsman borrowed from the US Coast & Geodetic Survey in Washington DC; most of OSE experts were on loan from US Government jobs. Fat Bob's hydrographic map drawings had contour lines crossing each other or simply tucked into any handy other contour line. Such never happens on river or sea bottoms.

Bob went along on the MARGA HENN voyage from Saigon to Cam Ranh Bay to draft up the hydrographic surveys onboard the ship. He was heavily armed with two .357 mm pistols. On one occasion when the survey motorboat returned to the ship after dark, they were greeted by Bob pointing a pistol at them – he's lucky he didn't get shot.

The Navy was puzzled by the disappearance of dozens of large steel mooring buoys in the harbor. Mike dove and found they were sunk from bullet holes;

Bob had amused himself during the day using them for target practice.

One weekend the MARGA HENN sailed up the seacoast to Nha Trang for a bit of 'R&R' – great beaches, restaurants and ladies. Returning late Sunday night to Cam Ranh Bay with Stu Agon at the helm, the ship strayed out of the buoyed channel and grounded on a sandbar. The tide was strong and going out.

As it would be an embarrassment for a hydrographic survey ship to run aground in their own mapping area, Dan and Mike swam four miles in the dark to shore to arouse a tugboat to pull the ship off. The swim hazards included sharks, sea snakes, and running into huge slimy floating jelly-fish, not to mention getting mistaken as VC sappers and getting shot by a US Navy patrol boat. The tugboat crew was awakened and by dawn's early light the MARGA HENN was safely at the dock – in time for breakfast at the Navy mess hall.

Below: A typical hydrographic survey drawing showing contours and bottom soil sample results.

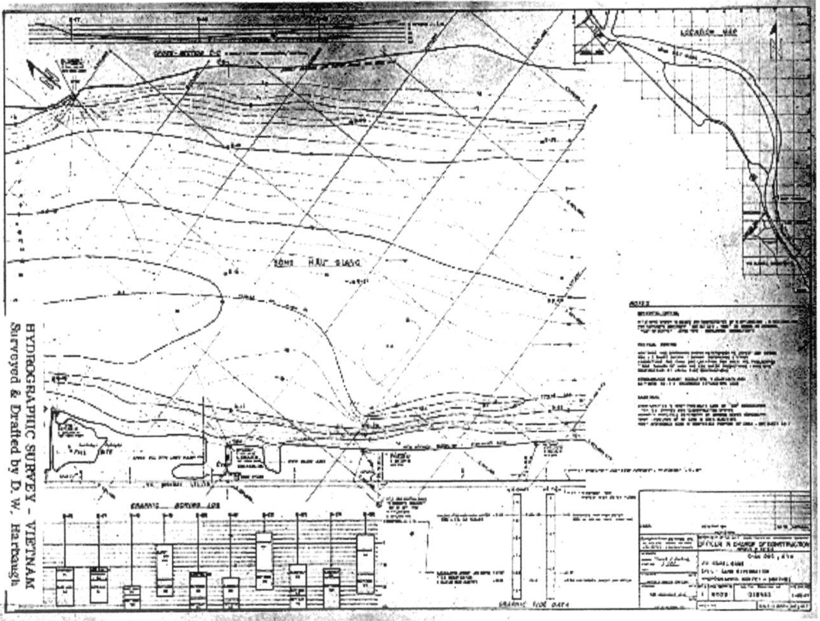

The Motor Ship MARGA HENN

The MS MARGA HENN was the private yacht of Dr. Max Henn, a WW II German officer who moved to Thailand after the war. Dr. Henn owned and ran the 'Atlanta Hotel' in Bangkok. In 1966 the Atlanta Hotel was a place right of the Hollywood movie 'Casablanca'– one wouldn't be surprised to see Humphrey Bogart and Ingrid Bergman saying "Play it again, Sam." During the fit-out of the MARGA HENN for Vietnam, Dan played the piano in the evenings at the Atlanta. Thanks to the internet in 2012, Dr. Henn's son contacted Dan for information on the fate of the MARGA HENN; and offered him his old job of piano player at the Atlanta.

Piano gig by Dan

"Run on conservative principles and imperiously heedless of fashions and trends, The Atlanta is untouched by pop culture and post-modern primitivism. Its style and atmosphere hark back to gentler and more cultivated times. The Atlanta is popular with cultured occidentals, with writers, academics, artists, cinema & theatre and other professional people, with dreamers and innocuous eccentrics ."

M. / S. "MARGA HENN"
for Charter to Parties,
Sightseeing Tours and
Weekend Trips.
For Reservation call **"The Atlanta Hotel",**
Bangkok, Tel. [illegible].

The MARGA HENN took a mortar round during the 1968 Tet Offensive and sank in the Saigon River. KADH then purchased the ship from Dr. Henn and raised it. Ian Blackman shown inspecting it. The ship was later converted to an offshore oil supply vessel.

Capt. Dan and M-3 ‘Grease Gun’ submachine gun on the MARGA HENN

At the end of the OSE contract, Dan wrote a letter to Willard Bascom detailing all the dumb things OSE management did on the contract.

OCEAN SCIENCE AND ENGINEERING, INC.
OCEAN SCIENCE BUILDING
4905 DEL RAY AVENUE
WASHINGTON, D. C. 20014

26 September 1967

Mr. Daniel W. Harbaugh
1550 W. Seventh Street
Long Beach, California

Dear Mr. Harbaugh:

Thanks very much for the Harbaugh report which I saw for the first time two days ago. It is a fascinating document and well-written; I only wish that I had seen it a year ago.

I was horrified to discover that you had not been properly paid and I immediately called our accounting department. Somehow it slipped through the cracks and I immediately had it and other possible mispayments investigated. We accepted your statements at face falue with the exception given in the attached statement from our accounting department. You are certainly entitled to the interest on the unpaid balance and you have my sincerest apologies, both for the general conduct of OSE during the time you were in Vietnam and for the time you were not paid properly.

You may be interested to know that when we changed managers to John Griggs, most of our problems evaporated and for the last six months we have done first class, efficient surveys that compare favorably with any in the world.

Yours truly,

Willard Bascom

Willard Bascom
President

KADH Force Vietnam

Near the end of the OSE 6-month Navy OICC contract, the Saigon dunces hadn't paid the crew for months. Dan politely notified OSE Project Manager Erlanger of this; Stu paid Erlanger a visit and stated he was going to "beat the shit" out of him if he didn't pay the past-due wages; he paid. This and other OSE incompetence convinced KADH they could do a much better job hydrographic surveying in Vietnam, and all quit OSE at the end of their 6-months Navy contract; with appropriate verbiage as to where they could "Shove it".

EXPLORATION SCIENCE INC.

After OSE, KADH members remained in Vietnam with the members taking individual positions with other major contractors.

Mike Kelly was the driving force in resurrecting KADH. In November 1968, Mike and Gary went to Alameda, California, to attend the 'Coastal School of Deep-Sea Diving'. They were joined by Dan, who had just completed a year in Vietnam with Pacific Architects & Engineers and was in California finalizing the sale of his ski lodge. Together they created 'Exploration Science Inc.', a California corporation. KADH reassembled, and now a legal entity, ESI went after a US Navy OICC contract for hydrographic surveying and soils coring; and got it. The KADH Force was increased with the addition of Larry Roberts, fresh out of Oklahoma State University, Ian Blackman, a young British sea captain; Ken Gaulden, formerly a new car salesman; Dudley 'Duke' Sager, ex-Army 82nd Airborne, and Stu's brother, Kirk Agon, a well-dressed slick talker, last employed as a parking lot attendant in Hollywood. Kirk's initial value was his access to a mimeograph machine in Hollywood; this was used to print travel orders to fly from California to Vietnam on Military Air Transport flights from Travis AFB - no one would suspect anyone deliberately wanting to go to Vietnam in this era of anti-Vietnam War demonstrations.

Traveling MATS was much more convenient than going 'Space Available' on over-crowded Pan American Airlines flights.

An entire Saigon 3-story building at 676 Phan Dinh Phung became KADH headquarters and housing.

The mission was to obtain a Navy contract. While Kirk was charming the OICC with regular house calls, Mike, Gary and Dan were off to Hong Kong and Singapore acquiring SCUBA diving gear, a Pirelli inflatable boat, a Boston Whaler boat and motors, Wild T-2 theodolites and surveying gear, a Fathometer, and everything else needed for hydrographic surveys. OSE had required a costly 'Mobilization Fee' on their contract; ESI was pre-mobilized at their own expense, and ready to work on short notice.

ESI chartered the Malaysian coastal freighter 'KERTANG' and Capt. Blackman and Mike sailed it to Saigon.

KADH's first project was to locate and salvage a cargo of 40-ft steel H-beams lost when the barge carrying them capsized several miles offshore Vung Tau in a big storm. This was a 'needle-in-a-haystack' search, but using the Boston Whaler with a magnetometer and positioning the boat with onshore theodolites making 5-minute fixes via hand radios, the steel was located late afternoon on the 2nd day – no small feat. It was too late to dive on it. The fix angles from the two theodolite stations recorded in standard surveying field books would enable return to the exact spot. But, Kirk Agon on one theodolite hadn't recorded anything in his record book, requiring another day to relocate the steel. What did he think he was supposed to be doing? That was Kirk's last venture into the field.

Dan went down in SCUBA gear to view the find, a jumbled pile of steel H-beams in 50-ft of water. He selected an H-beam and hooked the hoisting hooks on each end. Surfacing and signaling the winch operator, the H-beam was hoisted onboard the KERTANG. As it was getting dark and a storm coming, the KERTANG headed for the dock.

At anchor on the second night out just past midnight the ship was boarded by Vietnamese pirates; Sager was on watch duty and shouted the alarm. All hands jumped out of their bunks, grabbed their guns and ran on deck.

The pirates hastily retreated to their Chinese junk in the water below. They had thrown a rope-ladder with grappling hook over the ship's rail and had trouble untying the rope from their boat. In those few seconds, Ian Blackman picked up a large iron anvil from the deck and dropped it on the pirate's boat; it went right through the deck and hull and sank the pirate ship.

The pirates swam for their lives; whether they succeeded or not was unknown. The horrified look on the pirate's faces when they saw that anvil about to be dropped on them would have won an 'Oscar' in a horror movie. After this incident the night watch included a machine gun.

Having located the steel and proved it was there, the Navy decided it would be more expedient to use a big crane barge to salvage the rest of the steel.

ESI was amply paid for their one H-beam; but more important, it opened the door for a Navy hydrographic surveying contract. Thanks to Kirk Agon's socializing with OICC Naval Officers, including showing Lt. Goodspeed the impressive display of gear at 676 Phan Dinh Phung, plus getting him serviced by a local lady, the OICC announced calls for bids on a new 6-month contract. The bidding day arrived and Dan presented the ESI bid – about $1,029,000 in 2014 money.

Several hi-powered bidding competitors presented proposals, including OSE, Trans-Asia Engineering, and Asian International Laboratories. The OICC Admiral considered them all. He favored ESI because they had showed they knew what they were doing and weren't afraid to do it. Then he said there was no way he could justify awarding a contract to a firm with six expensive Americans on the field crew payroll, when the competitors needed only one or two and the rest were Vietnamese or 'TCNs' -Third Country Nationals.

Dan returned to KADH headquarters with the bad news.

ESI had a $30,000 ($210,000 in 2014 dollars) debt to investor friends of Gary who financed most of the mobilization expenses strictly on their trust in Gary and Kirk Agon.

Kirk Agon showed his true colors and disappeared without a word the next day back to the USA – skipping out on the tab.

Logically, city-slicker smooth-talking Kirk should have been the one to convince the Navy they should reconsider and award the contract to ESI. Dismayed but determined, Dan wrote the following letter to the Admiral took it to him and waited as he read it.

18 June 1969

RADM H.J.JOHNSON, Officer-In-Charge-Construction/RVN
Bldg. 176 Hai Ba Trung
Saigon

Dear Sir:

This is to inform you of a series of events that may cast serious doubts on the integrity of the U.S. Navy. The story is briefly this:

Exploration Science Inc. has actively solicited hydrographic survey work from OICC since December 1968.

In early May 1969 our Mr. Kirk Agon, Vice President, was informed by Lt. T.J. Regan of OICC Engineering that Exploration Science Inc. had been selected by the OICC Contractor Selection Board to supply two complete hydrographic survey units, including base vessels, equipment and personnel, for a contract to commence 1 July 1969. Lt. Regan again confirmed this in my presence.

Mr. Agon inquired specifically of Lt. Regan at the first notification of the selection if such notification was sufficient for us to proceed to secure the necessary vessel on charter, and Mr. Agon was assured it was.

In following conversations with Lt. Regan, Lt. J.W. Goodspeed, LCDR. M.S. Ely, and others , our selection as contractor to provide these two vessels was confirmed by their actions. Mr. Agon received no dissent when he stated he was leaving for Singapore, Hongkong, and the United States to charter vessels and purchase equipment to meet this contract. Mr. Agon then left on 16 May 1969 to do just that.

The following week, while attempting to get the Scope-of-Work on this contract, I was informed by Lt. Regan that we no longer were requested to furnish two vessels, but only one instead. It was apparent that Lt. Regan didn't relish the task of breaking the bad news. By sheer coincidence, Trans Asia Engineering held an "open house" aboard their vessel in Saigon the day before.

2

I should point out that we have a good idea of what Trans Asia, as our competitor, does, simply because the captain of our vessel, the M/V Kertang, was the captain of Trans Asia's vessel, the M/V Indian Ocean, and Trans Asia's chief hydrographic surveyor until recently was our Mr. Agon's brother. Nothing unethical was involved in this situation.

While we could find no fault in Lt. Regan's explanation of " competition ... best interests of the government .." etc., and in our own knowledge that Trans Asia does a satisfactory job, we still were left with the rather expensiveeproblem of un-chartering a vessel, de-recruiting personnel, and cancelling equipment orders. But, fair enough, we'll accept our one boat contract and let it go at that.

Lt. Regan directed us to proceed to Mr. Billman's office in OICC Contracts, and a Scope-of-Work was obtained. A proposal was submitted several days later. We were informed this proposal was too high for the money scheduled, and a second proposal was submitted. The second proposal was accepted as within the range of the funding, and this proposal was presented and discussed with Mr. Billman's office, Lt. Goodspeed, and Lt. Regan. At no time was there any indication that it was unacceptable

1400 hrs. 18 June 1969 was scheduled by Mr. Billman's office for "contract negotiations". Present were myself, representing Exploration Science Inc., Mr. Charles Hyde, representing Asian International Laboratories, as our subcontractor for soils work, and Cdr. I.D. Crowley, representing the OICC, with Lt. Goodspeed, Lt. Regan, and others in attendance.

The "Contract Negotiations" lasted about five minutes, and included no negotiations what-so-ever. Cdr. Crowley opened by saying our proposal was "excessive", refused to designate what parts he felt "excessive", refused to negotiate on any portion of the proposal - in spite of my statement that I was there to negotiate on any and every item, and ended with the statement that, in view of the short time remaining before the contract starting date of 1 July , there was no time to negotiate further, and that the "second selection" of the Contractor Selection Board - who just happened to be Trans Asia - would be requested to undertake the contract.

3

We don't deny the Navy's right to seek the best value for the taxpayer's money - in fact we will even insist on it - but, we do deny their right to use Exploration Science Inc. as the goat to justify this supposed quest for economy. Our proposal was available material for OICC reading for several weeks prior to this 18 June negotiations farce. Any comments on excessive prices would have been more appropriate then.

It was our intention to furnish what was required on this contract at a competitive price. The Scope-of-Work is vague enough for several interpretations. We came to the negotiations table with one interpretation. We were prepared to negotiate on others.

In failing to get this contract, after spending considerable time, money and effort directly in reliance on statements made by personnel of OICC, we have been considerably damaged. We intend to pursue this matter to the satisfaction of all who should be concerned, including ourselves, a responsible level in the United States Navy, and the United States Government.

This letter is our first step - to indicate our reactions to OICC. We will next advise our feelings to the proper investigative authorities, and we will next advise our feeling to the proper legislative authorities. We will review the possibilities of recourse.

It is not my intention to create a problem for the U.S. Navy, the press seems illustrated with more than enough now, but to all appearances someone in the organization in being "influenced" beyond the call of duty. I suggest you find that man before I do.

Yours very truly,

Daniel W. Harbaugh, President
Exploration Science Inc.
Box 4216
Pasadena 91106

Duly impressed, the Admiral held new contract negotiations on July 1, 1969. Lt. Goodspeed spoke up and said ESI was a team and all essential to fast accurate hydrographic surveys anywhere in Vietnam. Some minor adjustment, having Asian International Laboratories as an ESI sub-contractor for soils testing, and the day ended with awarding ESI the 6-month contract, – much jubilation at 676 Phan Dinh Phung!

NAVFAC 4280/1 (7-66)
Supersedes NAVDOCKS 1337
S/N 0104-814-0000

LETTER CONTRACT

CONTRACT N63185-69-C-4168

ENGINEERING SERVICES FOR HYDROGRAPHIC SURVEY

SUPPORT FOR DREDGING AND RELATED WORK

VARIOUS LOCATIONS,RVN

EXPLORATION SCIENCE, INC.
(Contractor)

NAVAL FACILITIES ENGINEERING COMMAND
DEPARTMENT OF THE NAVY
WASHINGTON, D.C.

N63185-69-C-4168
LETTER CONTRACT

(d) The definitive contract resulting from this letter contract will include a negotiated firm fixed total price which in no event is to exceed ONE HUNDRED FORTY SEVEN THOUSAND DOLLARS ($147,000.00).

The Contractor shall specifically identify those items of effort that are to be performed by subcontract. All subcontracts amounting to $10,000 or over will require prior approval by OICC RVN. It is further understood that the Contractor's proposal and cost or pricing data on which the negotiation of this contract is based, must fully comply with Public Law 87-653, commonly known as the "Truth in Negotiations" law, as implemented by ASPR and DPC No. 66. Promptly after negotiation of definitive price, the Contractor agrees to submit a DD Form 633-1 and backup data reflecting the negotiated price and cost elements making up the negotiated price.

UNITED STATES OF AMERICA

By [signature]
W. J. FRANC[illegible], [illegible] USN

For Commander, Naval Facilities
Engineering Command
Contracting Officer

ACCEPTED this 1st day of July 1969
EXPLORATION SCIENCE, INC.
By [signature]
(Signature)

DANIEL W. HARBAUGH, President
(Typed Name and Official Title)

Engineering Services - $147,000.00

This $147,000 contract would be at least a $1,029,000 in 2014 dollars. The contract was "not to exceed $147.000", with a required mid-point accountability for work performed. Kirk Agon, who would not work in the field, was presumably compiling the report in the office. Dan arrived in from a survey mission a week before the mandatory submission date and found Kirk had done nothing. As ESI operating expenses and payroll had been considerably exaggerated to provide repayment to the investors, Dan had to hastily 'cook the books'. Ian, Larry, Ken and Sager were handed big back-dated paychecks, to cash and return the money to Gary.

DEPARTMENT OF THE NAVY
OFFICER IN CHARGE OF CONSTRUCTION
NAVAL FACILITIES ENGINEERING COMMAND CONTRACTS
REPUBLIC OF VIETNAM
FPO SAN FRANCISCO 96626

30 June 1969

Dear Sir:

This is a letter of introduction for the Exploration Science, Inc. soils exploration team under the direction of Mr. Daniel W. Harbaugh. This team is under contract to the Officer in Charge of Construction, Republic of Vietnam, under contract number PII N63185-69-C-4168, for soils exploration work in the III and IV Corps areas. Exploration Science, Inc. is an invited U. S. Contractor.

Any assistance which you may wish to give in insuring the safe and effective conduct of their operations in your area is appreciated. Inquiries should be addressed to the AOICC for Dredging, OICC RVN. (Tiger 3336, ext. 238/9.)

Very respectfully,

JACK P. CAMPBELL
By direction

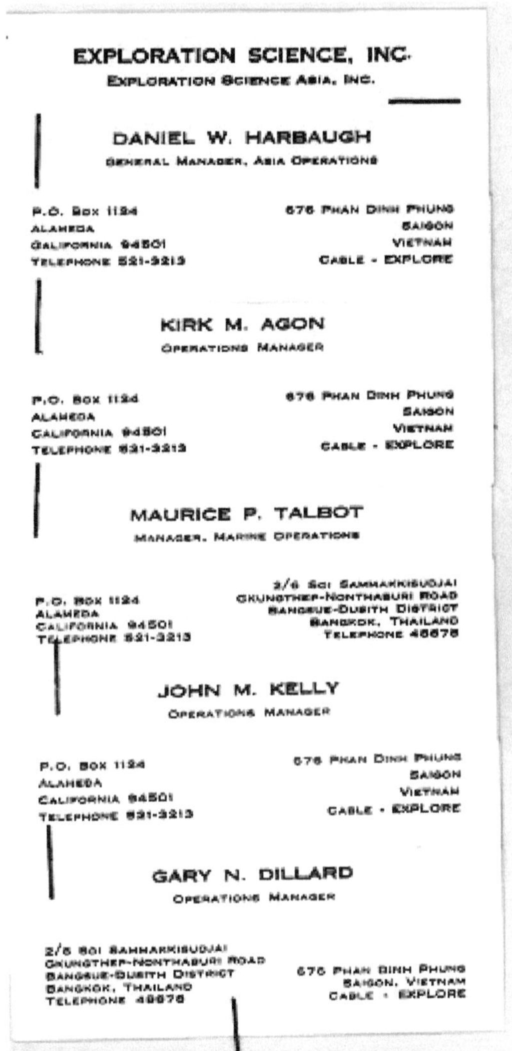

EXPLORATION SCIENCE, INC.
EXPLORATION SCIENCE ASIA, INC.

DANIEL W. HARBAUGH
GENERAL MANAGER, ASIA OPERATIONS

P.O. BOX 1124
ALAMEDA
CALIFORNIA 94501
TELEPHONE 521-3213

676 PHAN DINH PHUNG
SAIGON
VIETNAM
CABLE - EXPLORE

KIRK M. AGON
OPERATIONS MANAGER

P.O. BOX 1124
ALAMEDA
CALIFORNIA 94501
TELEPHONE 521-3213

676 PHAN DINH PHUNG
SAIGON
VIETNAM
CABLE - EXPLORE

MAURICE P. TALBOT
MANAGER, MARINE OPERATIONS

P.O. BOX 1124
ALAMEDA
CALIFORNIA 94501
TELEPHONE 521-3213

2/6 SOI SAMMAKKISUDJAI
KRUNGTHEP-NONTHABURI ROAD
BANGSUE-DUSITH DISTRICT
BANGKOK, THAILAND
TELEPHONE 46675

JOHN M. KELLY
OPERATIONS MANAGER

P.O. BOX 1124
ALAMEDA
CALIFORNIA 94501
TELEPHONE 521-3213

676 PHAN DINH PHUNG
SAIGON
VIETNAM
CABLE - EXPLORE

GARY N. DILLARD
OPERATIONS MANAGER

2/6 SOI SAMMAKKISUDJAI
KRUNGTHEP-NONTHABURI ROAD
BANGSUE-DUSITH DISTRICT
BANGKOK, THAILAND
TELEPHONE 46676

676 PHAN DINH PHUNG
SAIGON, VIETNAM
CABLE - EXPLORE

Maurice Talbot, a deep-sea diving expert, was the ESI representative based in Alameda, CA.

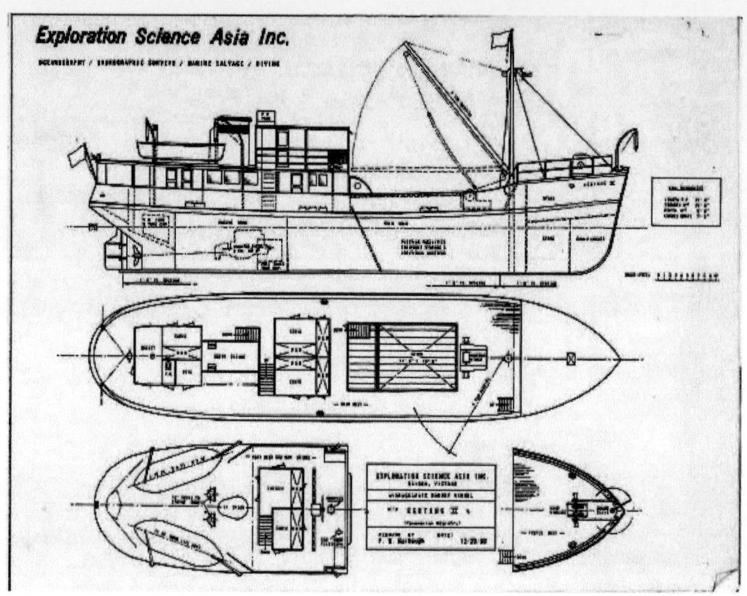

MV KERTANG

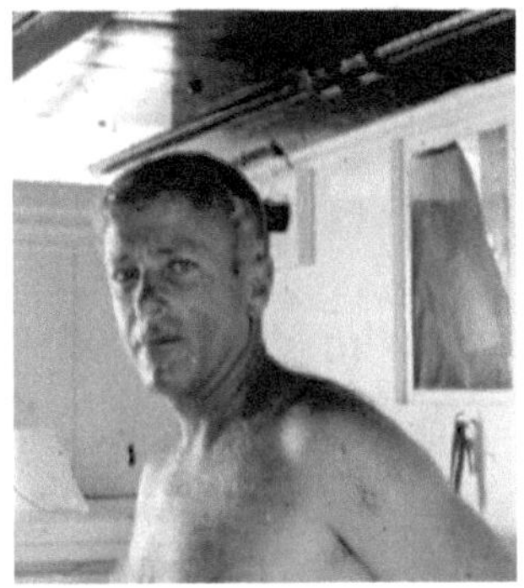

Dan onboard KERTANG

Below: Ian Blackman and his two talking parrots 'Ralph' and 'Fred'; both quite accomplished in profanity.

Sager, Gary and Stu onboard KERTANG

Ian, Kirk, Mike and Ken – 'Muster on the foredeck'

Mike, Stu and Dan using fathometer in Boston Whaler. On one occasion after completion of a survey up a small river, Mike was water skiing back behind the Boston Whaler and ran into a firefight between the ARVN on one river bank and the VC on the opposite bank. Both sides were so surprised and amazed they stopped firing; with Mike waving 'Hi' as he skied through.

Gary, Ken, Sager and Mike onboard KERTANG; AJAX II alongside.

Capt. 'Bilge' Blackman at the helm of KERTANG

Below: Chief Engineer and Cook relaxing on voyage Singapore to Vietnam

Gary, Mike and Dan on KERTANG.

Mike and Dan on maintenance squad on KERTANG

Gary and Dan on KERTANG

Towing the AJAX II on the Tangong

Mike in Hong Kong buying the Motor Launch AJAX II.

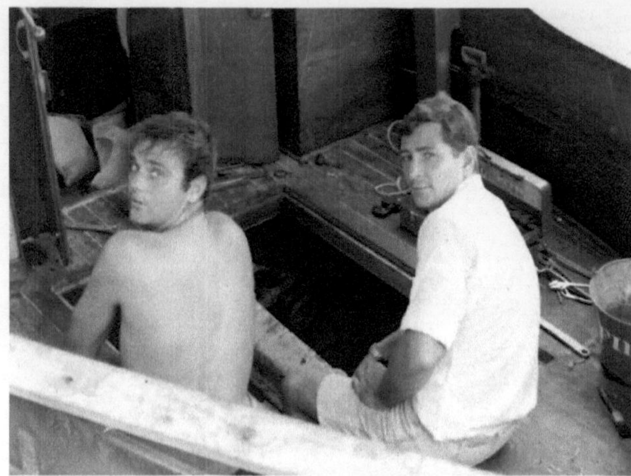

Ian and Mike onboard AJAX II in Saigon

Sager onboard AJAX II

Dan – ‘Speak no’; Larry – ‘Hear no’; Sager –‘See no’.

Below: The ‘Enforcers’ – Sager, Larry, and Gary.

The ESI Executive Staff off to the Saigon International House for dinner: Larry, Gary, Kirk, Ian, Sager

. Below: Ian and Sager with the Boston Whaler and an Army M151 Jeep - 'liberated' from the US Army. Many surveys were conducted by small boat hauled behind a Jeep to remote rivers.

Ian, Sager and Larry

Below: Larry, Ian and Dan

Dan, Mike and Gary in Singapore 1968. Below: Houston 2014

Kirk and Gary, Sager headed for the Lovely Bar in Saigon. All KADH members had Honda-50 motorcycles; but they never quite hit the density of the native bikers.

Dan and local Saigon lovely at the Lotus Bar.

Kirk Agon – KADH 'Best Dressed'.

Ian charming a Vietnamese pot-belly pig.

Below: Dan with Ian's pet kitty cat.

Ian and his adopted family in Saigon.

Ian out surveying on an exceptionally hot day; clothes optional.

On numerous days it was so hot the survey crew had to cool off in the river. This was hazardous due to floating missiles from river village sewage outfalls.

Kirk and Ian at the 'CORDS' office in Chau Doc. CORDS was a special 'Civil Operations and Revolutionary Development Support' group operating independently from the U.S. Military; President LBJ's pet project to "Win the minds and the Heart of the Vietnamese people." Dan later went to work for CORDS as 'Chief, Engineering Division, Military Region II'. MR II, referred to as 'Two-Corps', covered Vietnam from above Saigon to Nha Trang and all of the Central Highlands, including Dalat.

'Van', ESI's lovely Secretary in the Saigon office

Larry gets smoke bombed on a survey positioning station.

"Would you fellows hold the noise down ... we're trying to run a survey here."

Larry, Sager and Ian, and spectators in the Mekong Delta

Below: Conference in the Mekong Delta. L-to-R: RMK-BRJ dredging rep, Kirk, Ian, Dan.

ESI Coring vessel

Ian on soils coring site in Mekong Delta

Larry and Dan at a river crossing ferry.

Ian on positioning station for soils coring.

.Ian, Sager and Larry on shore positioning station.

Larry and Sager doing a survey at a Mekong Delta Swiftboat base. John Kerry was at a base like this.

Below: Dan and Ian resting on a Vietnamese grave site – often the only high ground in a swamp.

Dan with new motorboat at Saigon office.

Dan in Hong Kong

Below: Larry, Sager and Ian at a river survey site hotel.

Dan on soils coring in Mekong Delta.

.

KERTANG on Saigon River

Morning muster at KADH villa.

Morning street sweepers on the road to the river.

ESI kept up to date with the latest hydrographic surveying technology.

EXPLORATION SCIENCE INC., 676 Phan Dinh Phung, Saigon

ZIG-ZAG PROFILING WITH THE HONEYWELL S-1301-A5 SONAR

Zig-Zag Profiling is so named because of the zig-zag path resulting when the Honeywell Profiler is set to cross-section at right angles to the course of the moving sounding boat. The skew of the cross-section is governed by the speed of the sounding boat during the 15 seconds taken to make the sonar sweep. Radio coordinated "fixes" are taken by shore station theodolite at each end of the sweep, enabling the cross-section to be located accurately on the plotting sheet.

In addition to the cross-sectioning sonar, a conventional single line sonar, such as the Raytheon DE-719 Recording Fathometer, is used to record the profile of the boat's track down the range line. This center-line profile gives a continuous check on the cross-section profiler as it passes the vertical position directly under the boat. The chart recordings from both sonars are used to make an accurate contour map.

In the accompanying sketches an example of a Zig-Zag survey in 20 meters average depth water is shown. The Honeywell Profiler is set to sweep through 140°, or 70° from vertical on each side of the boat's track. For maximim accuracy, only 60° from vertical is utilized as the extent of coverage. The depth of water controls the distance out in the extent of coverage. In this case the 20 meter water depth allows about 35 meters out each side of the range line, or a total swath of about 70 meters. Therefore, the shore control ranges are set at 70 meters apart.

The sonar "rays" at the 70° limit from adjoining range lines will overlap, in this case by about 40 meters, allowing for corrections to these greater angle rays from the more accurate lesser angle rays from the adjoining range line.

The Zig-Zag method provides thorough coverage at a rapid pace, Saturation coverage can be obtained by slowing the sounding boat to a minimum forward speed.

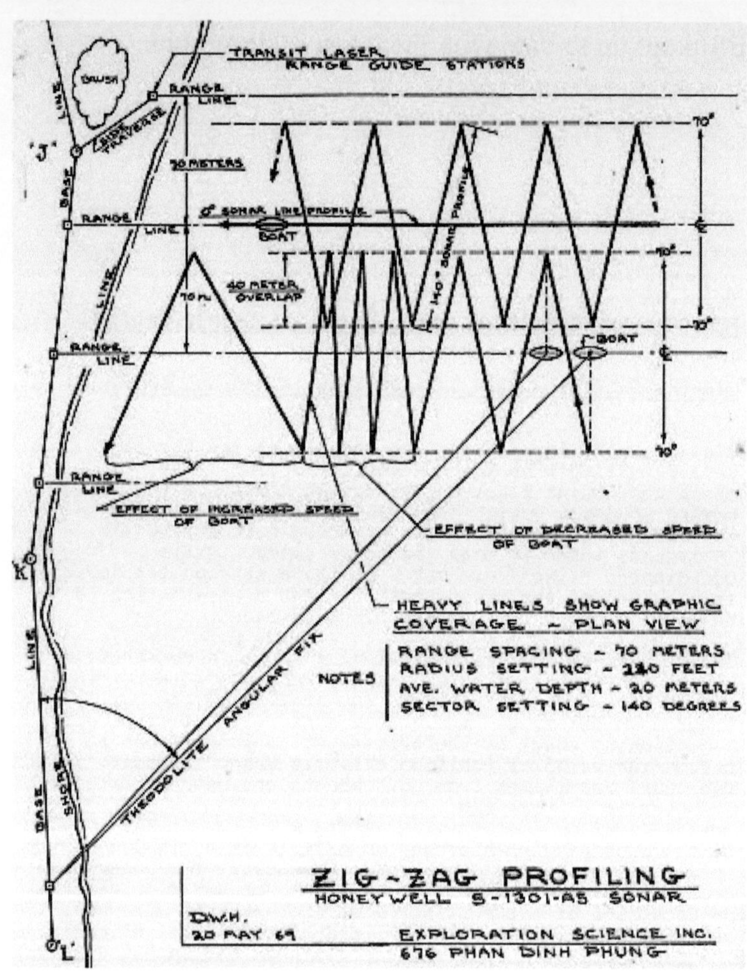
TRANSIT LASER
RANGE GUIDE STATIONS
BRUSH
RANGE LINE
'J'
BASE LINE
30 METERS
RANGE LINE
0° SONAR LINE PROFILE
BOAT
140° SONAR PROFILE
40 METER OVERLAP
70 m.
70°
RANGE LINE
BOAT
RANGE LINE
EFFECT OF INCREASED SPEED OF BOAT
EFFECT OF DECREASED SPEED OF BOAT
'K'
HEAVY LINES SHOW GRAPHIC COVERAGE - PLAN VIEW
NOTES
RANGE SPACING - 70 METERS
RADIUS SETTING - 210 FEET
AVE. WATER DEPTH - 20 METERS
SECTOR SETTING - 140 DEGREES
THEODOLITE ANGULAR FIX
SHORE
BASE LINE
ZIG-ZAG PROFILING
HONEYWELL S-1301-AS SONAR
D.W.H.
20 MAY 69
EXPLORATION SCIENCE INC.
676 PHAN DINH PHUNG
'L'

FINALE - KADH

The Navy contract had run for four successful months when Kirk Agon unexpectedly reappeared at 676 Phan Dinh Phung in Saigon, and demanded to rejoin KADH, and get on the contract payroll. All during the execution of the contract Gary had been the very efficient and essential Saigon office manager, handling the financing, payroll and all transport and equipment needs; plus going out in the field on river hydrographic surveys and soils corings on the Vietnamese 'Chinese Junk' drill-ship. Gary, like all KAHD members except Kirk, was never chicken about the possibility of getting shot or blown up. As Kirk had been a key salesman in getting the contract, he was reinstated in KADH. He was expected to sell the Navy or USAID on a new contract, plus help out in the field. He did neither and, again, showed his colors. The straw that broke KADH's back was Kirk's proclamation that he, as the self-styled key-man in ESI, was entitled to a majority 55-percent of ESI ownership; and Dan, Mike and Gary would get 15-percent each. This arrogance convinced Dan and Mike they wanted nothing more to do with Kirk. Kirk made his announcement in Dan's office; Dan picked up a small survey notebook and made motion to throw in at Kirk. Kirk turned white and ran. KADH dissolved and Mike and Dan moved on to other ventures in Vietnam.

FINALE – EXPLORATION SCIENCE INC.

Gary and Kirk continued on as Exploration Science Inc. in the business as owners and operators of tug boats and barges in the in the Mekong Delta and in Dong Ha just south of the DMZ. They purchased the 126 foot ex-US Navy minesweeper 'MV HECATE' and contracted it to the Military Sealift Command as a tug boat in the Mekong Delta. They also contracted services to Global Marine and Shell for offshore petroleum drilling support during the start up of the first exploration of oil off the coast of Vietnam.

The MARGA HENN was resurrected and renamed 'CRESPO '. The superstructure was new and the wooden hull clad in steel.. A 12V71 Detroit Diesel engine was installed.

Gary and Kirk got out of Vietnam just as the country fell to the communists. Kirk left the last day by helicopter to an aircraft carrier waiting offshore.

Global Marine owed them $13,000 ($91,000 in 2014 dollars) on invoices for marine services. Gary flew to the Global Marine office in Cairo, Egypt, to collect on the invoices and was informed Kirk Agon had already been there and collected the money.

Kirk absconding with the company funds ended ESI; and Gary will probably be inclined to shoot him if they ever meet again.

POSTSCRIPT - KADH

Mike Kelly - The 'K' in KADH .

After KADH/Exploration Science Inc., Mike went to work with Oceaneering Inc.; starting as a Diving Supervisor and Explosives Expert; then on to being Country Manager of Operations in Columbia and then Africa.

Mike later joined in the formation of 'Undersea Associates, Ltd.' in Aberdeen, Scotland, for a project to salvage the German warships sunk at Scapa Flow in WW I. Dan later joined the firm.

Per Google: "The German cruiser MARKGRAF was scuttled in Scapa Flow. 20 August 1979. The wreck is to be salvaged by Undersea Associates Ltd.
Source; Lloyd's List, 15 August 1979. 31 January 1980. Salvage operations have been completed."

Mike and Dan at their desks in Aberdeen

Valid Seismic Data in 4' Water?

Meeting this fabled craft in a jungle swamp wouldn't seem unusual to the seismic crews of THE EXPLORATION GROUP LTD. The crews, equipped with the HODGAIR Air/Mud Gun System, onboard the M/V "RIVEREX I" and other specialized craft, go where others cannot .. in water shallow as 3½ feet ... to obtain valid seismic data.

The HODGAIR System is proven in action in Indonesia. Data comparisons to prior surveys by explosives show superior results, including depths of penetration, by the HODGAIR Air/Mud Gun Energy System.

Alert Interested Go-Anywhere Personnel .. Accurate Survey Positioning Methods, such as the Motorola RPS-3 System .. Digital Field Data Recording .. In-House Data Processing, including an SDS Sigma 7 48k Digital Computer ..... These sum to optimum value for the Exploration Dollar. Making a comparison with standard on-shore shallow water methods, THE EXPLORATION GROUP offers a 30 to 1 Cost Advantage ...

The Exploration Group was a spin-off of Undersea Associates in partnership with Paul Hodges, a noted geophysicist in Singapore and inventor of the 'HODGAIR Air/Mud Gun Energy System'- an economical alternate to using explosives.

Mike is now 'Tri-Zen', a profitable consultancy based in Singapore.

"**TRI-ZEN** is a consulting and advisory business established in 2000, which has a primary focus on the energy industries in Asia.

The business has team of more than 30 lead consultants, mostly seniors from the energy industry and with extensive experience of business in Asia. The team has deep knowledge of most aspects of the energy business, including particularly fuels and lubes marketing, trading & risk management, LNG and power, and upstream project evaluation and development.

The business provides services in strategic consulting, business development, project execution, training and organization development. In addition to oil, gas and power, it also covers areas as diverse as chemicals, water and industrial gases.

Clients include major international and national energy companies, regional business conglomerates, investment houses and global professional services businesses. The business has been profiled on CNBC 'Managing Asia' and our consultants frequently provide expert commentary on energy related issues in regional news programmes.

We offer experienced and cost effective professional guidance. We provide quality independent and confidential services. While responsive to client needs and able to meet most challenges, our main areas of focus are.

Business Development

Strategic Services

Organisational Development

TRI-ZEN is headquartered in Singapore and has a presence in countries throughout Asia."

Stu Agon – The 'A' in KADH

Stu left the firm after completion of the OSE Navy contract. He was a loner and never an organization man. He remained in the Far East after the Vietnam War, became an English teacher in Vietnam and, at last report, is in the Philippines.

Kirk Agon replaced Stu as the 'A' in KADH in the ESI Navy contract; the 'A' soon stood for one rotten Apple. After the Navy contract, Kirk and Gary continued on as ESI. After Kirk departed Vietnam and absconded with the ESI company funds, he reportedly became a banker with Chase in Washington DC; presumably they kept the bank vault locked. "Treachery, though at first very cautious, in the end betrays itself." Titus Livy

Gary Dillard - The 'D' in KADH.

After completion of the ESI Navy contract and dissolution of KADH, Gary partnered with Kirk and continued as ESI in the tug and barge business until Vietnam fell. Gary was active with World Vision International in rescuing the boat people after Vietnam fell.

From 1990-2005 Gary formed and operated the SCUBA diving company 'Seadive Adventures Pte. Ltd., Singapore'. With their 52-ft twin-turbo diesel dive boat 'LORD JIM', they ran over 300 3-day dive trips with 8-10 persons to the Tioman Islands off the coast of East Malaysia. Mike Kelly joined in on many of the trips and helped out with the dive training.

KADH Force Vietnam

Gary's older brother has operated a machine shop in Canton, Ohio, for the past 50 years. In 2006 they opened a Vietnam subsidiary in Binh Duong near Saigon. Gary supervised the creation of this 10,000 sq.ft. facility with 25 machinist employees, and wrote the 'SOP' - Standard Operating Procedures. However, Gary's heart was never in the technical trades; he soon plans to spend the rest of his active days onboard the LORD JIM cruising to South East Asia tropical islands, including Bali.

Dan Harbaugh - The 'H' in KADH. Dan went on to career as a Civil/Military Engineer in Vietnam and afterwards with the US Army Mideast Div., and then with the 'Multinational Forces & Observers', the peace-keepers in Sinai, Egypt. He is now retired in Houston, TX.

Trade Hazards

In November 1967, Dan was 'Chief, Engineering, Military Region II' and was inspecting the EMD diesel power plant at Dak To in the Central Highlands when the 'Battle of Dak To' began. This was a major engagement in the Vietnam War; PAVN rockets and shellfire destroyed aircraft, the base's ammunition dump and fuel depots. In addition to the bombardments, there were small enemy sapper squads roaming the base. All US non-combatant personnel were issued M16 rifles and assigned a position; with shoot anything that moves. Dan was in the 'TOC' bunker. He got out on the third day with a convoy. The battle lasted 3-weeks, with 376 US killed and 1,441 US wounded.

On one occasion, Dan was inspecting road construction by ARN Jeep with ARN driver on a narrow country road to Song Mao. Ten black pajama-clad heavily armed Vietnamese stepped out of the tall elephant grass, blocked the road and held up their hands in 'STOP !' They didn't know who Dan was, nor Dan know who they were; there were Vietnamese pajama-clad 'Popular Forces' on our side. Dan had bought a box of 'Rum Crook' cigars at the Phan Thiet P-X ; he got out of his Jeep, walked up the line putting a cigar in each man's mouth; went back down the line lighting each cigar with his 'Bic' lighter; lit one for himself and got back in the Jeep. Somewhat amazed, they moved to the side of the road and beckoned 'Go on'.

Vietnam Performance Evaluation

PACIFIC ARCHITECTS & ENGINEERS, INC.
APO San Francisco 96307

• EMPLOYEE PERFORMANCE EVALUATION •

Prepare this review in accordance with the instructions on the reverse side.
YOUR SUPERVISORY JUDGEMENT IS REFLECTED IN THE EVALUATION YOU MAKE OF OTHERS

NAME [illegible] EMP. NO. [illegible] DOH 24 February 1970

1. VOCATIONAL KNOWLEDGE: General technical knowledge related to occupational skill, and ability to apply theory effectively to practical situation.

( )	( )	( )	(XXX)	( )
Marginal understanding of the job. Limited proficiency.	Adept at job, requires only minimal instruction. Above average.	Job knowledge is sufficient to satisfy job requirements. Average.	Versatile & self-sufficient. Competent in all aspects of the job.	Inadequate knowledge & skill. Requires continuous guidance. Unsatisfactory.

REMARKS: EXCELLENT [illegible], [illegible], [illegible].

2. INITIATIVE: Ability and willingness to perform effectively in the absence of supervision or specific instructions.

( )	(XXX)	( )	( )	( )
Acts independently on routine matters. Normal supervision required.	Decisive & resourceful. Sound judgement, good self-starter.	Seeks solutions independently. Little guidance necessary.	Reluctant to act without specific guidance. Lacks self-confidence.	Generally unsatisfactory. Close supervision necessary.

REMARKS: LITTLE OR NO SUPERVISION REQUIRED. INITIATES MORE THAN REQUIRED ON A ROUTINE BASIS.

3. PERFORMANCE: Amount of work accomplished under routine conditions, based on the minimum requirements of the position.

( )	(XX)	( )	( )	( )
Slow or erratic in useful work accomplished.	Consistently exceeds standard job requirements.	Above average in the production of useful work.	Cannot fulfill normal job requirements. Unsatisfactory.	Adequate to maintain normal volume of work.

REMARKS: GREAT MASS OF WORK [illegible]. ACCEPTS ANY [illegible] TASK.

4. QUALITY OR WORK: Accuracy, thoroughness and dependibility of work, based on the minimum requirements of the position.

( )	( )	( )	(XX)	( )
Not conscientious; errors are frequent & serious.	Frequent errors & often untidy. Marginal.	Exceptionally neat & accurate. Monitoring unnecessary.	Generally precise & neat. Only a few errors noted.	Usually acceptable. Neat with occasional errors.

REMARKS: [illegible] DEADLINES. [illegible] AND [illegible].

5. ADAPTABILITY & ATTENDANCE: Consider adjustment to job requirements, work environment, and general attendance record.

( )	( )	(XX)	( )	( )
Good attendance, Adjusts well to any job & general environment.	Poor attendance. Difficulty coping with general conditions, personnel & customs.	Excellent attendance record. Adapts rapidly & smoothly to changing conditions.	Satisfactorily adjusted to present situation; accepts changes reasonably.	Sporadic attendance record. Resists change & reflects some discontent.

REMARKS: [illegible]
EASILY ADJUSTS.

6. PERSONALITY & APPEARANCE: Cooperation, attitude toward work & colleagues, personal hygiene, and general public projection.				
( ) Dresses well. Tolerant & Well liked. Appears satisfied.	( ) Fair appearance. Exhibits some discontent. Irritative.	(XX) Well groomed. Very cooperative; liked & respected. Enjoys job; congenial.	( ) Poor appearance. Creates friction & dissatisfaction. Cannot communicate	( ) Good appearance. Usually agreeable; has normal Staff relations.
REMARKS: NEAT AND CLEAN. EXCELLENT ATTITUDE. ON OWN INITIATIVE IMPROVED PHYSICAL FACILITIES FOR ALL EMPLOYEES.				

7. SUPERVISORY ABILITY: General leadership potential; ability to plan, organize and effectively manage subordinates. (OMIT RATING IF A NON-SUPERVISOR)				
( ) Unsatisfactory. (Fully justify this rating in the remarks section.)	( ) Poised, aggressive; plans for all contingencies. Takes positive action to develop staff.	( ) Supervises routine activities without trouble; weak in staff relations.	( ) Plans & assigns work well. Achieves objectives without undue difficulty.	(XX) Capable & well organized. Competent in staff relations & production.
REMARKS: MANAGES THRU QUIET RESOURCEFUL LEADERSHIP. HIGHLY COMPETENT IN PLANNED ORGANIZATION.				

8. SUPERVISOR'S GENERAL COMMENTS: (Use addendum sheet if this space is insufficient.)
QUALIFIED FOR HIGHER POSITION.

9. EMPLOYEE'S COMMENTS: (Attach detailed memorandum of rebuttal if you disagree with the evaluation, or if this space is insufficient to reflect your view

10. SIGNATURES AND DATES: (All signatures must include the typed name of the individual)

IMMEDIATE SUPERVISOR: GEORGE V. OTT	Date: 7 JUNE 1970
EMPLOYEE [illegible]	Date:
INSTALLATION OR DEPARTMENT MANAGER GEORGE V. OTT	Date: 7 JUNE 1970
DISTRICT MANAGER	

From Remarks:

" EXCELLENT TECHNICAL KNOWLEDGE ... WELL QUALIFIED ... HIGH PERFORMANCE "

" LITTLE ON O SUPERVISION REQUIRED ... INITIATES MORE THAN REQUIRED ON A ROUTINE BASIS "

" GREAT MASS OF WORK PERFORMED ... ACCEPTS ANY DIFFICULT TASK "

" MEETS DEADLINES ... THOROUGH AND DEPENDABLE "

" MANAGES THRU QUIET RESOURCEFUL LEADERSHIP ... HIGHLY COMPETENT IN PLANNED ORGANIZING "

" QUALIFIED FOR HIGHER POSITION "

Per George V. Ott , Col. USAF , Ret.

DEPARTMENT OF THE ARMY
ENGINEER LOGISTICS COMMAND
APO 09697

MELJI 11 June 1979

SUBJECT: Letter of Appreciation

Mr. Dan Harbaugh
Supervisor Fac. Engr.
Pacific Architects & Engineers
Khamis Mushayt, Saudi Arabia

Dear Mr. Harbaugh:

I want you to know how very much I appreciate the super job you are doing at Khamis Mushayt. I fully recognize that your personal efforts and professionalism have been the drawing force to dramatically improve support accomplishment for the Southern Area Office. Although you had to contend with severe handicaps such as an ill-defined scope of work, significant separation from your Area Manager, and an extremely adverse situation created by your predecessor, you personally took charge and turned the situation around.

I have great confidence that you will continue to provide the best possible efforts at Khamis. You also have developed a sense of reliability and accomplishment within the community, and have actively worked to improve even further the responsiveness and effectiveness of your staff.

Please accept my personal thanks for your direct and personal contributions. My one regret is that there is no comparable position to yours at Tabuk for which I could ask for your reassignment to my new location.

Sincerely,

Benjamin W. Graham

BENJAMIN W. GRAHAM
MAJ CE
Commander, ELC-Jidda

DEPARTMENT OF THE ARMY
U.S. ARMY ENGINEER DIVISION - MIDDLE EAST
RIYADH DISTRICT, CORPS OF ENGINEERS
WESTERN AREA OFFICE (PROVISIONAL)
APO NEW YORK 09697

MECWA 3 June 1980

SUBJECT: Letter of Appreciation

Mr. Daniel M. Harbaugh, 330486
Facilities Engineer Supervisor
Pacific Architects and Engineers, Inc.
Jidda, Saudi Arabia

Dear Mr. Harbaugh:

On 3 June I will be departing the United States Army Engineer Division-Middle East after serving two years as Deputy District Engineer, Jidda District and Area Engineer, Western Area Office (Provisional). During this period, Jidda District reached its peak manning level with more than 1,000 personnel and their dependents; completed over one billion dollars of priority construction for the Ministry of Defense and Aviation; and, as the work load diminished, was deactivated on 1 April 1980 with the Western Area Office created to complete the remaining work at Tabuk and Khamis Mushayt.

I would like to take this opportunity to single you out personally for the contributions which you have made as Facilities Engineer Supervisor. Through your positive attitude, dedication, professional competency and cooperation, essential mission and life support services were maintained at a level of excellence in which we all took great pride. Your outstanding performance of duty allowed the United States Army Corps of Engineers to accomplish one of its most dynamic and challenging construction missions in its 205-year history.

Please accept my appreciation for a job well done. It has been a privilege for me to have served with you. I wish you continued success in all your future endeavors.

A copy of this correspondence has been furnished your Area Manager for inclusion in your official personnel records.

WILLIAM B. WILLARD, JR.
LTC, Corps of Engineers
Area Engineer

Dinner with Saddam Hussein: When the Iraq/Iran War began Iraq flew numerous civilian aircraft to Khamis Mushayt Air Base in Saudi Arabia for safe-keeping. Dan accompanied a delegation to Bagdad to arrange for aircraft arrivals and crew accommodations. Saddam hosted a dinner and shook hands with all attending.

The KADH Crew:

Duke Sager, Ian Blackman, Ken Gaulden and Larry Roberts all rightfully earned the rank of 'Honorary KADH Members'.

Dudley 'Duke' Sager returned to Michigan and became a well-paid construction union worker. He is now retired.

Two KADH crew members went on to be Vice-Presidents in the international shipping world.

Ian Blackman

"Ian Blackman, BAX's new vice president, Ocean Freight, Asia-Pacific, will lead the development of Asia to U.S. trade lanes. Blackman is based in Hong Kong."

Ken Gaulden

"Kenneth C. Gaulden, Senior Vice President and Director, Maersk Line, Limited. Mr. Gaulden has been with Maersk Line, Limited since 1999."

Larry Roberts

"Larry Roberts, Experienced Transportation Executive. CSX Intermodal, Inc.; Sea-Land Service, Inc.; Maersk Line."

Larry is now retired in Florida.

Larry on 'FaceBook' - 2014

All the mentioned gentlemen, excluding Kirk Agon, were in Vietnam for the adventure, with getting rich incidental. They proved loyal comrades, resourceful, can-do confident and had the guts to work in the field with warfare going on around them. The Vietnam War had only a few major battles, but had the constant hazard of ambushes, land mines, snipers and sappers blowing up anything handy. The enemy was indistinguishable from the Vietnamese populace. The KADH field forces regularly ventured into 'unsecured' territory where they were on their own.

Duke Sager summed up the adventure with his statement:

"This war is hell, but it's better than no war at all."

Miscellaneous KADH Tales

In the February 1967 Dan arrived from the field at the KADH Saigon headquarters at 676 Phan Dinh Phung, and went to bed. About midnight all Hell broke loose with explosions and gunfire. Dan grabbed his M-3 submachine gun,'Grease Gun', and rushed to the rooftop ready to start shooting. All the KADH gang were there, seeming unconcerned; and then they explained this was Tet, Chinese New Year, being celebrated with firecrackers and shooting off guns. The sky over Saigon was filled with glowing tracer bullets, such that any aircraft wouldn't stand a chance.

The Lovely Bar

The Lovely Bar in Saigon was a favorite evening destination for the KADH gang. The proprietor, MamaSan Hoa, knew every member by name and always welcomed them. In addition to the regular and available 'Saigon Tea Girls', she had a beautiful young daughter, Teresa, who helped tend the bar. All hands were warned Teresa was off-limits for any romantic notions. Teresa took a fancy to Mike and lost her maidenhood. When MamaSan Hoa found out she was furious; she called Mike every name in the English and Vietnamese swear-book and would have beaten Mike up had the rest of KADH intervened. Such were the hazards of night life in Saigon.

Sunday Excursion

One Sunday the KADH Force sailed to Hòn Tre, an inland where Stu, in his Special Forces days, had cached a huge supply of weapons, C-4 explosives, grenades and smoke bombs in a cave. Retrieving all this, the gang spent the day shooting and blowing up about everything in sight, including the former French fort. The island now uninhabited except for a few sheep herders at the opposite end, and they, wisely, stayed out of sight. In late afternoon an Army spotter plane flew over. The next day the Army daily newspaper 'Stars and Stripes' reported a big battle on the island. Since no military commander could dare admit he didn't know about the battle, the report was unchallenged

The Boarding Party

The MARGA HENN, a white yacht sailing up the China Sea coast in the middle of the night, when there was no other traffic, attracted a Vietnamese Navy patrol boat with a US Navy Lieutenant onboard. The patrol boat approached completely blacked-out; suddenly it shined a blinding spotlight and fired a barrage of tracer-bullets across the MARGA HENN's bow, as in 'STOP !'. The ship stopped and the Navy Lt. boarded. He relaxed upon seeing the Americans and after being informed of the mission, he noted the ice machine onboard. As his Vietnamese Navy craft had nothing but warm water to drink, he ended up trading cartons of C-rations, ammunition and grenades for a tub of ice cubes and two cases of Coca Cola.

As he climbed back aboard his patrol boat, he looked up and was shocked to see Stu on the on the top deck with a machine gun ready to blow his patrol boat out of the water; Stu had been there all the time.

The Coca Cola Incident

One of the first tasks Capt. Dan assigned the new crewmen in Saigon Harbor was to take all the empty cases of Coca Cola, consumed on the voyage from Bangkok, to the Saigon Coca Cola bottling plant on the river for a deposit refund, which they could keep. Mike and Stu loaded the Boston Whaler with the empty cases and disappeared around a bend in the river. They came back quickly minus the cases. Dan was quite impressed with their efficiency. Months later Dan asked how much they got in the refund, and was informed they merely went around the river bend and dumped all the cases overboard - KADH members don't waste time on such trivialities.

The Doll

Dao, the normally quiet, very efficient but not too good-looking housekeeper at 676 Phan Dinh Phung, had a crush on Gary. Gary, a noted man-about-town with the ladies, paid no attention to her, but did give her a cute little doll, which she placed in a prominent place and cherished. One evening the peace was shattered as Dao let out a big scream; the gang, figuring something drastic had happened, rushed to her. Still screaming and yelling in Vietnamese, she pointed to the doll – Mike had equipped it with a big penis made from C-ration potatoes. Mike was a bad boy.

KADH Motor Pool

Just prior to the Navy contract, a Special Forces friend parked a military Jeep convenient for Gary to 'liberate'. As all US Military vehicles had to carry a 'Trip-Ticket' authorizing their use, upon arrival at the KADH villa, Dan painted the entire Jeep black with a white stenciled number on the bumper to resemble an Army 'CID' , Criminal Investigation Div., Jeep, which no MP ever challenged. A Vietnamese policeman noticed the painting going on and a half hour later the villa was surrounded by Vietnamese police. The Police Chief, rightly, thought the Jeep was stolen, and ordered a policeman in his white uniform to drive it away. Everything on the Jeep was wet paint, including seats and steering wheel. The driver, with black paint all over him, started to get out, but was ordered back in, and drove it away. The Police Chief said he would release the Jeep upon proof of ownership. As KADH had no such proof, the Jeep was gone.

ESI later acquired two 'mislayed'M-151 Army Jeeps. These were painted yellow and white with 'Military Lines of Communication' logo on the spare tire cover. Since no MP knew what this was, the Jeeps were never challenged for Trip Tickets.

Communications

Whereas OSE had trouble-prone 'Radio Shack' hand radios, Special Forces contacts provided ESI with the great AN/PRC 77 radio transceiver nicknamed the 'Prick-77'. This was a 'combat-net' radio enabling ESI field crews to monitor any nearby enemy engagements – very handy when the fighting got too close for comfort. On one survey a nearby Army unit was annoyed by ESI monopolizing the radio band with survey boat radio fixes every few minutes – such as "Five four three two one ... Mark Bravo", and broke in "This Sergeant Smith ... get off this radio." Mike replied "This is Colonel Kelly, you get off the radio." ... "Sorry SIR!" Special Forces contacts also provided combat-rations, machine guns, ammo, grenades and anything else adventuresome young lads might find useful.

Street Clearing

Major streets in Saigon had Vietnamese Army gun posts in the middle of intersections, and after curfew they fired randomly down the street to keep the streets clear. On one occasion they were shooting down KADH's street, Phan Dinh Phung. Just to liven things up, Stu threw a hand grenade off the balcony and for the next few hours the gun posts at each end of the street fired at each other.

The Paper Route

The readers may rightly ask how and where such a young renegade group as ESI, prior to any Navy contract revenues, got the capital to fund chartering and outfitting a survey vessel, purchase expensive surveying equipment, and have a Saigon villa for headquarters. The answer, in brief, was from investors utilizing the 'Paper Route' – currency manipulations.

To prevent the enemy from getting US dollars, the military issued Military Payment Certificates, 'MPC', in lieu of dollars for any in-Vietnam payments to troops. Military regulations required troops to exchange their MPC for Vietnamese Piasters for local purchases. There was legal exchange rate for MPC to Piasters; however the Vietnamese marketplace would give about 3 times the legal rate to get their hands on military MPC. Vietnamese bars accepted MPC in lieu of Piasters and accumulated vast quantities, with no officially legal way to convert it to it to US dollars. They would trade two MPC dollars for one greenback dollar. A G.I. or authorized civilian could take MPC he bought at one-third price and cash it in at a military banking facility for full value in US dollars. In the early days of the Vietnamese War, any G.I. or American with ID could walk up to any military currency exchange desk, such as while departing at Saigon Airport, with $10,000 MPC, or any amount they could logically explain if asked, and exchange it for US dollars. The net result was enterprising Americans created a very profitable MPC gathering system from the Vietnamese holders.

The KADH Vietnamese lady landlord at the Saigon headquarters, a 3-story building at 676 Phan Dinh Phung, was well connected in the Catholic Church. Vietnamese Catholic priests would arrive on their Honda 50s with thousands of MPC dollars in money belts under their black robes. The major investor in ESI, an American RMK-BRJ construction supervisor and good friend of Gary and Kirk, would be there, collect all the MPC, and return a few days later with US dollars. He loaned ESI $30,000, about $210,000 in 2014 dollars, to fund fledgling ESI during the expensive pre-contract mobilization period; with, naturally, expectations of repayment with a profit.

The military eventually became aware of the MPC manipulations and the new regulations specified only $200 MPC could be exchanged for dollars at military banking facilities; this temporarily slightly curtailed the MPC operations.

The military overlooked the Army Post Offices 'APO's, where a properly ID'd person could exchange $1000 MPC for ten $100 US Postal Money Orders. All money orders required entering the name of the recipient during purchase, and were typically mailed home to the USA.

The investors gave KADH money orders to pay for purchases in Hong Kong and Singapore. Dan was a long-time checking and banking customer of the Hong Kong & Shanghai Bank in Los Angeles from his California ski lodge construction and operating days; LA bank Vice-President J. Patrick Smith was a skier and good friend. With a letter of introduction from Smith, presenting a big stack of postal money orders for cash at the Hong Kong branch, with a recipient's name on each, was no problem; the banker merely asked "You know all these people?" ...."Certainly."

,

WANTED

Information on theft or diversion of US Government property, blackmarket activities, and illegal currency transactions involving US military personnel, civilian employees, contractors, or contractor employees.

Such information is vitally needed to preserve and protect US interests. Confidences will be respected.

SENT TO
VICTOR FRIZBEE
Box 1000
APO 96222 (In Country)

ATTENTION: VICTOR FRIZBEE

Are you aware that : The U.S. Embassy USAID, OICC and MAC-V are the major offenders of currency regulations. If, indeed, you desire to preserve and protect U.S. interests, then investigate their methods of paying certain Vietnamese Contractors holding U.S. Dollar banking accounts outside RVN ; the Embassy's method of paying the rent on the international house; the U.S. army's method of payment for leasing certain Vietnamese Hotels and Villas, presently being used as billets ; etc... or, are these agencies considered « above the law » ?

ATTENTION: VICTOR FRIZBEE - Notices in the Saigon paper . As the investors in Exploration Science Inc. were occasionally currency violators, Dan felt obligated to refresh Frizbee on reality.

Purchasing Agents

During the ESI mobilization period most purchases were made in Hong Kong or Singapore. As traipsing all over town to accumulate the wide assortment of equipment needed was impractical, Gary found and befriended a smart reliable purchasing agent in each place. The Agent was briefed on taking payment in US Postal Money Orders, thus avoiding explaining same to individual merchants. Whether it was Wild T2 theodolites, tool kits, motor boats, Rolex watches, etc., all was gathered in one place for inspection followed by shipment to Saigon.

KADH REUNION – Houston, TX, 26 May 2014

Now some 48 years after the original KADH creation, KADH assembled once again for a reunion in Houston,TX. Mike Kelly - 'K', arrived from Singapore; Gary Dillard - 'D', arrived from Vietnam; Dan Harbaugh - 'H', Houston; ESI crewmen Duke Sager arrived from Michigan, and Larry Roberts arrived from Florida; both Honorary KADH members. Duke Sager, noting the original KADH meeting "A gathering of eagles", dubbed the reunion as now "A gathering of old turkeys."

Sager, Mike, Dan, Gary

Editor's Note

Most of the photographs in this book are from up to 48-year old 35mm slides. They have been computer-enhanced as much as possible. The personages in this book are likewise about 48years older; beyond computer-enhancing. Exploration Science Inc. is still listed as a California corporation; who knows what it could have become in the oceanographic and geophysical business today?

"Bid good-by to sweetheart, bid good-by to friend;
The Lone Trail, the Lone Trail follow to the end.
Tarry not, and fear not, chosen of the true;
Lover of the Lone Trail, the Lone Trail waits for you."

Dan Harbaugh – June 2014

ADDENDUM

ESI Losses in the fall of Vietnam:

Items ESI lost during the fall of Saigon, included four Datsun pickups, one Toyota Land Cruiser pick up, one Mazda 1500 Sedan, the hydrographic surveying instruments and numerous other equipment.

The 1,000 HP M/V HECATE was under a Military Sealift Command contract at $750.00 per day. The 500 HP M/V BOORPHAR VI was under a MSC contract at $450.00 a day. The ESI two small 250 barges were under MSC Contract at USD 55.00 each a day. All were lost.

Monetary loses on 'Cancelled due the convenience of the US Government' contract clauses totaled about $460,000. The claim supporting documents never got out of the APO (Army Post Office) for submission.

Without going into the 'CPA' mode and translated into 2014 dollars, ESI lost over USD $1,000,000 in the fall of Vietnam.

ADDENDUM – Exploration Science Asia Inc.

Exploration Science Asia was a spin-off of ESI created to serve the Asian civilian market.

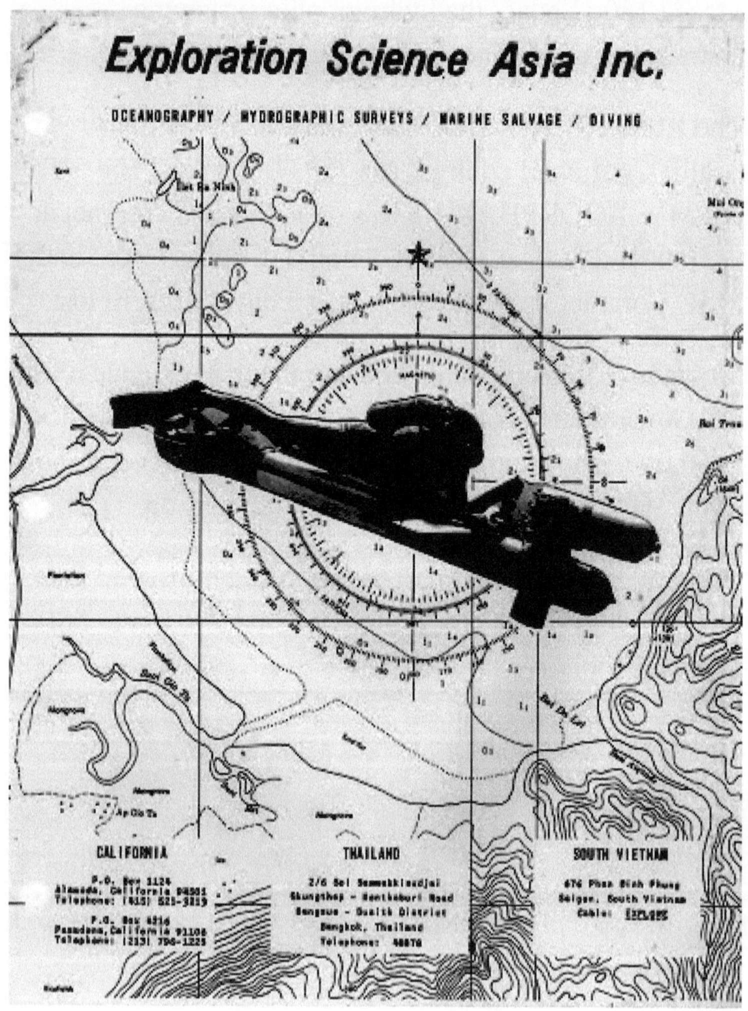

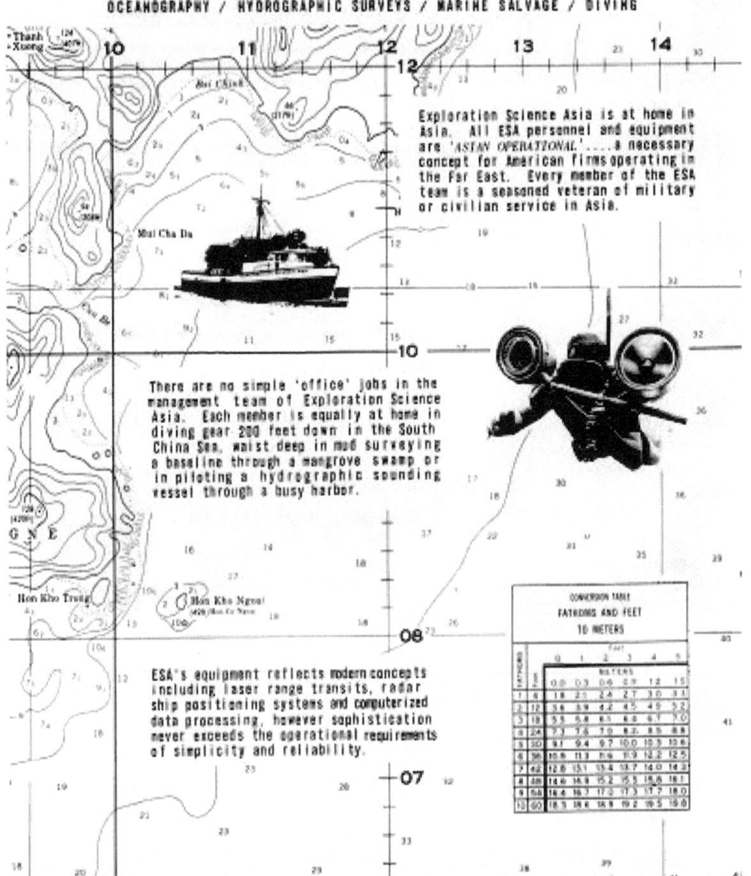

FATHOMS	FEET	0	1	2	3	4	5
		0.0	0.3	0.6	0.9	1.2	1.5
1	6	1.8	2.1	2.4	2.7	3.0	3.3
2	12	3.6	3.9	4.2	4.5	4.9	5.2
3	18	5.5	5.8	6.1	6.4	6.7	7.0
4	24	7.3	7.6	7.9	8.2	8.5	8.8
5	30	9.1	9.4	9.7	10.0	10.3	10.6
6	36	10.9	11.3	11.6	11.9	12.2	12.5
7	42	12.8	13.1	13.4	13.7	14.0	14.3
8	48	14.6	14.9	15.2	15.5	15.8	16.1
9	54	16.4	16.7	17.0	17.3	17.7	18.0
10	60	18.3	18.6	18.9	19.2	19.5	19.8

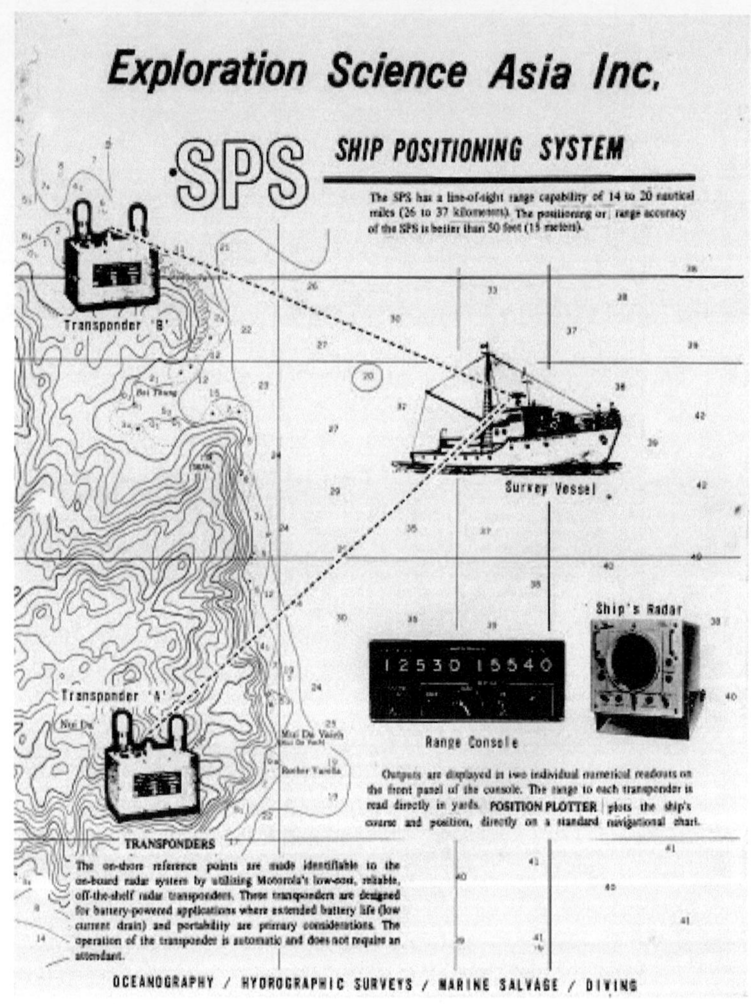
Exploration Science Asia Inc.
SPS
SHIP POSITIONING SYSTEM
The SPS has a line-of-sight range capability of 14 to 20 nautical miles (26 to 37 kilometers). The positioning or range accuracy of the SPS is better than 50 feet (15 meters).
Transponder 'B'
Survey Vessel
Ship's Radar
1 2 5 3 0 1 5 5 4 0
Range Console
Outputs are displayed in two individual numerical readouts on the front panel of the console. The range to each transponder is read directly in yards. POSITION PLOTTER plots the ship's course and position, directly on a standard navigational chart.
Transponder 'A'
TRANSPONDERS
The on-shore reference points are made identifiable to the on-board radar system by utilizing Motorola's low-cost, reliable, off-the-shelf radar transponders. These transponders are designed for battery-powered applications where extended battery life (low current drain) and portability are primary considerations. The operation of the transponder is automatic and does not require an attendant.
OCEANOGRAPHY / HYDROGRAPHIC SURVEYS / MARINE SALVAGE / DIVING

Exploration Science Asia Inc.

Capabilities ...

THE SPS TEAM

For off-shore and large area hydrographic surveys where manned on-shore survey control stations are impractical or hazardous, ESA operates with the Motorola Ship Positioning System - SPS. This system utilizes the survey vessel's X-band radar with on-shore reference points made identifiable by radar transponders. A Range Console presents a visual and printed numerical readout of the distance from the vessel to each transponder. Triangulation from this data fixes the vessel's position while the recording fathometer indicates the depth.

The extent of survey coverage is indicated automatically to the helmsman by a Position Plotter that plots the vessel's course trace on a suitably scaled and orientated coastline chart, such as a standard navigational chart.

SPS has a line-of-sight range capability up to 20 nautical miles with a positioning accuracy within 50 feet. The simplicity and reliability of the SPS, its adaptability to any shipboard radar without modifications to same, and its unmanned easily concealed, expendable if necessary, on-shore transponder units, make this positioning system " Asian Operational".

ESA is in the process of adapting the SPS and sounding systems to computer operations whereby the shipboard data will be taped for direct conversion to contour maps, cross-sections and quantities by the computer. This system will eliminate the usual data processing, reduction and drafting work.

The basic SPS system will be operational aboard the ESA diesel auxillary sloop in Spring 1969 for off-shore surveys. It may be transfered to shallow-draft craft for delta area surveys.

OCEANOGRAPHY / HYDROGRAPHIC SURVEYS / MARINE SALVAGE / DIVING

Exploration Science Asia Inc.

Capabilities ...

THE TRANSPAC TEAM

The ESA "Transpac Team" is an oceanographic team based aboard a Columbia 50' diesel auxillary sloop, a sister ship of the 1967 Transpac Race winner. This new all-fiberglass vessel, while also a thoroughbred oceangoing yacht, is a capable hydrographic survey base vessel. The fiberglass maintenance-free construction, its sailboat independence from fueling and mechanical problems, and its ample accomodations make it "Asian Operational".

For hydrographic surveys the normal ship's compliment is six men - a four man survey team and two ship's crewmen. Where applicable the survey is conducted using two aluminum boats - a 17' sounding boat and a 14' liaison boat to coordinate tide, range and tracking stations. The sounding boat uses a Raytheon DE-119D Recording Fathometer, is guided on range by an on-shore LT-2 laser transit or by sight targets, and is tracked with on-shore Wild Theodolites on radio coordinated 30 second intervals. Calculating, data reduction and drafting facilities are available aboard the base vessel, but will generally be processed in the Saigon office due to more optimum conditions.

The base vessel carries shallow-water diving gear, including air compressor, and dives to 50 feet are normally a part of any contract. Dives over 50 feet are subject to charges determined by the conditions involved. All team members are qualified divers.

The Transpac Team is self-sufficient and requires no customer shore support, however it may be to the customer's advantage to further the water work by providing shore survey personnel, shore transportation, and shore data processing facilities.

The basic Transpac Team plus deep-water diving gear will be available aboard the ESA 75' diesel motor vessel for heavy diving operations.

OCEANOGRAPHY / HYDROGRAPHIC SURVEYS / MARINE SALVAGE / DIVING

Exploration Science Asia Inc.

Capabilities ...

THE FLYING SQUAD

The ESA "Flying Squad" is a four man hydrographic survey team designed for deployment by air to any site. All equipment, including sounding boat and motor, is portable and may be hand carried in one unit by the team if necessary. This team should be specifically considered for rapid water work on harbor and similar surveys. To further this concept the customer should provide all land based survey control as directed by ESA. Data reduction and drafting can be accomplished by customer under ESA supervision, by ESA personnel in customer facilities, or by ESA at the Saigon or Bangkok main office.

Basic team equipment includes a Raytheon DE-119D Recording Fathometer, weight 46 lbs.; a 14' Avon Inflatable Skiff, 80 lbs.; a Johnson 4 hp. outboard motor with 3 gallon tank, 45 lbs.; Wild T-2 Theodolite, field radio communications and other equipment as conditions require.

Customer should provide living and support facilities where available, however the team can be self-sufficient if necessary. This team is operational and available after 1 December 1968 on 14 day notice.

OCEANOGRAPHY / HYDROGRAPHIC SURVEYS / MARINE SALVAGE / DIVING

Exploration Science Asia Inc.

Capabilities ...

MARINE SALVAGE and DIVING OPERATIONS

ESA salvage and diving operations will be based aboard a sea-going steel barge. This barge may be towed by commercial tug to any site in Southeast Asia. Attendant vessel for local barge movements and diver tending is an LCM-6.

The barge contains the operation field office, living quarters, machine shop facilities, and complete diving and salvage equipment. The barge may serve as a base for hydrographic surveys using the LCM-6 and aluminum skiffs as sounding vessels. ESA anticipates the acquisition of a sea-going salvage tug in the near future.

Salvage equipment aboard the barge includes salvage pumps, jetting pumps, air compressors, winches, beach gear, hoisting gear, pneumatic tools, surface and underwater welding and cutting gear - including arc, oxy-arc, oxy-acetyl, and oxy-hydrogen.

Diving equipment includes SCUBA, shallow and deep-sea gear, helium-oxygen gas bank, recompression chamber, underwater communications, underwater television and photographic equipment.

All ESA personnel are qualified divers. Salvage Master Maurice P. Talbot is experienced in helium-oxygen dives at 420 feet. Underwater Demolitions are the specialty of Operations Manager John M. Kelly, a graduate of the U.S. Army Demolitions Engineering School. Operations Manager Gary N. Dillard heads a mobile SCUBA Shallow-Water Team which may be deployed by air to any site for underwater demolitions, salvage and recovery, and construction and inspection diving.

OCEANOGRAPHY / HYDROGRAPHIC SURVEYS / MARINE SALVAGE / DIVING

Exploration Science Asia Inc.

ESA MANAGEMENT PERSONNEL

DANIEL W. HARBAUGH - General Manager Asian Operations

B.S. Geo-Physics ... Land Surveyor ... Commercial Pilot NAUI Certified Diver ... Master of oceanographic motor vessel and Chief of Field Operations Harbor Surveys in Vietnam 1966.

MAURICE P. TALBOT - Salvage Master

Graduate U.S. Navy School of Deep Sea Diving, Washington. Commander, Burmese Navy, Retired ... Master Diver ... 20 years sea experience in Asia.

KIRK M. AGON - Engineering Operations Manager

B.S.E.E. ... NAUI Certified Diver ... Commercial Pilot 3 years marine and electronic experience in Vietnam.

JOHN M. KELLY - Hydrographic Operations Manager

Graduate Coastal School Deep Sea Diving, Oakland, Calif. NAUI Certified Diving Instructor ... Veteran U.S. Army Special Forces Vietnam ... Graduate Army Demolitions Engineering School ... Senior Hydrographic Technician on Harbor Surveys in Vietnam 1966.

GARY N. DILLARD - Diving Operations Manager

Graduate Costal School Deep Sea Diving, Oakland, Calif. NAUI Certified Diving Instructor ... Veteran U.S. Army Special Forces Vietnam ... Graduate Special Forces Underwater Demolitions School ... 2 years Marine Operations experience Vietnam.

OCEANOGRAPHY / HYDROGRAPHIC SURVEYS / MARINE SALVAGE / DIVING

ADDENDUM

Dan's Mission at Undersea Associates

"My primary mission was to develop hydrographic mapping services. The Port Of Sines, Portugal, had a problem – portions of their breakwater suddenly destructed without any apparent reason. As part my studies in Ocean Engineering class at Cal. State Long Beach, I had researched a similar occurrence; in 1933 portions of the Long Beach breakwater suddenly destructed for no apparent reason. The Long Beach weather was clear and calm, a gambling ship 3-miles offshore merely noted a passing smooth swell, fishermen on the breakwall saw a momentary slight rise in the water level, yet the portions of the breakwater disintegrated before their eyes, huge cut-stone blocks tumbling into the ocean.

Years later, wave studies showed the destructive force was wave orthogonals caused by a large moving mass of water, such as a tsunami after an earthquake, hitting a sea-bottom mound or obstruction and temporarily splitting. In compliance with the laws of physics, 'Momentum in = Momentum out'; the result was a narrow high-energy mass of water traveling at high speed and hitting the breakwater in one spot. Successive orthogonals from the same mound hit different portions of the breakwater. The Sines breakwater was constructed of concrete 'tetrapods' , similar in shape to a 'jack' in the children's game of Jacks. These tetrapods interlock as they are placed and resist most storm damage.

I wrote a proposal to the Port Of Sines Authority, detailing the Long Beach incident, and proposing a hydrographic survey to locate any possible offending mounds on the sea bottom within a few miles of the breakwater; we could accomplish this with a small boat using side-scan sonar. With too many other 'expert' opinions from their other consultants, the Port Authority wasn't convinced on our then far-fetched 'orthogonal theory', and no contract resulted.

Years later, I had the pleasure of reading an article in 'Engineering News Record' on the new discovery of orthogonals as the probable cause of the Port Of Sines breakwater damage."

"Edge B.L. et al (1982) Failure of the breakwater at Port Sines, Portugal, ASCE, Coastal Eng. Res. Council."

ADDENDUM: G-Ocean

Undersea Associates had great plans for branching into offshore geotechnical services; but it was too soon for this market.

"The best-laid plans of mice and men oft go astray."

Robert Burns

PRELIMINARY PROSPECTUS

for the formation of

GEOTECHNICS-OCEAN LTD. (G-OCEAN)

An offshore geotechnical services group to be organized, operated, managed and marketed by

UNDERSEA ASSOCIATES (UK) LTD.
Aberdeen, Scotland/Houston, Texas

with participation offered to

OFFSHORE SUPPLY ASSOCIATION LIMITED (OSA)
(DDG Hansa/VTG Bremen) W. Germany

and

PREUSSAG MEERESTECHNIK
W. Germany

PREFACE

This preliminary prospectus is for informal consideration by prospective venture participants and investors. A formal proposal detailing participation arrangements, business organization, personnel profiles, hardware descriptions, operating techniques, capital requirenents, operating costs and projected profits will be presented when appropriate.

INTRODUCTION

UNDERSEA ASSOCIATES LTD. proposes to establish an offshore geotechnical services organization, to be formed as an independent business entity with incorporation in such country or countries most advantageous to the venture participants and the markets sought. The organization,* tentatively titled GEOTECHNICS-OCEAN LTD., to be known as G-OCEAN, will acquire the OSA Survey-Drilling Vessel BERLINERTOR, modify the vessel as required for efficient downhole coring, organize a competent operating/management team, and aggressively market the vessel in coring and geotechnical services from UNDERSEA ASSOCIATES' offices in Aberdeen, Scotland and Houston, Texas.

VENTURE PARTICIPANTS

This preliminary G-OCEAN proposal envisions three principal venture participants, plus possible outside shareholders. In brief, UNDERSEA ASSOCIATES will provide the management; OFFSHORE SUPPLY ASSOCIATION will provide the BERLINERTOR; and PREUSSAG MEERESTECHNIK will provide geotechnical hardware and related services. G-OCEAN personnel will be drawn from participant firms where applicable and available.

UNDERSEA ASSOCIATES' primary objective is to provide an independent consultancy in the best interest of their clients and, as such, are not orientated towards the ownership of any specific offshore hardware. However, an ownership position in G-OCEAN is deemed sufficiently outside the primary undersea related consultancy and not in conflict. Further, as innovative undersea hardware designers, UNDERSEA ASSOCIATES will utilize G-OCEAN as a medium for field work on new developments for their clients.

OFFSHORE SUPPLY ASSOCIATION will profit from this venture by putting the presently under-utilized BERLINERTOR to work.

PREUSSAG MEERESTECHNIK's participation in G-OCEAN is desirable due to their geotechnical expertise and previous experience with the BERLINERTOR. PREUSSAG MEERESTECHNIK's participation in G-OCEAN may seem as self-competition; however, they can anticipate a great increase in utilization of their equipment and services in world markets, including coastal United States, due to the marketing ability of UNDERSEA ASSOCIATES. Further, G-OCEAN proposes to concentrate on deep penetration coring - and access to this expertise will enhance PREUSSAG MEERESTECHNIK's own portfolio of capabilities.

GEOTECHNICAL SERVICES

Deep Penetration Coring

Offshore 'geotechnical services' encompass many related specialties, some simple, some sophisticated. G-OCEAN proposes to concentrate on deep penetration offshore soils coring - a specialty simple in theory, but difficult to accomplish. This type coring, the process of boring and sampling downhole with a rotary drilling rig, provides the seafloor penetration, the quality of soil sample, and the attendant information universally acceptable for offshore foundation design. Since the offshore environment rarely affords the ideal coring conditions, such as a risk-free, stable, fixed-position work site, offshore coring is a high cost item to the client and, correspondingly, a high profit opportunity for an efficient coring contractor.

The major geotechnical firms, such as FUGRO and McCLELLAND, are usually inefficient in offshore coring, but compensate for this shortcoming by revenues from their undisputed expertise in sophisticated laboratory testing procedures and soils engineering. G-OCEAN, initially, proposes not to compete for this post-coring technology market, but rather to acquire these geotechnical majors as G-OCEAN clients by offering them coring services more profitable to use than their own.

G-OCEAN coring services will include onboard standard field testing of samples (soil description, torvane, minature motorized vane, pocket penetrometer, unconfined compression, unit weight, etc.) ; sample preparation for transport; and a written report with events log, boring log, sample data, and preliminary sub-bottom soils evaluation.

p.4

Coring Related Services

G-OCEAN proposes to offer all offshore geotechnical services practical and profitable within the overall BERLINERTOR deep penetration coring operations. These services will include remote sensing, such as bottom and sub-bottom profiling, magnetrometry, side-scan sonar and underwater television; on-the-bottom techniques, such as vibro-coring, penetrometer and in-situ vane; oceanographic procedures, such as precise water depths and current metering; and onshore and offshore positioning control surveying. Revenues from these services are projected as minor in comparison with downhole coring revenues.

Undersea Capabilities

In geotechnical projects there is often the requirement to get 'wet' - per project scope-of-work, or unscheduled emergency. The geotechnical majors are rarely qualified to accomplish this. UNDERSEA ASSOCIATES provides G-OCEAN with a built-in underwater capability. By illustration, in addition to accomplishing the remote sensing, physical oceanography, and shallow and deep penetration coring on a developing country harbor improvement project, G-OCEAN can conduct diver inspection and NDT testing of existing underwater structures, and explosive demolition of underwater obstructions.

Post-Coring Technology

G-OCEAN's major efforts will be expended on the BERLINERTOR coring operations - the greatest overhead expense and prime revenue source. Initially, until such time as profitable, onshore post-coring technology, such as sophisticated soils testing and soils engineering, will be subcontracted to outside laboratories and consultants. UNDERSEA ASSOCIATES has close relations with many high credential geotechnical consultants with offshore industry prominence. The client will be afforded the opportunity to utilize in-house, outside, or G-OCEAN consultants for post-coring technology.

Most large oil companies and other offshore constructors have in-house personnel or available consultants capable of accomplishing their post-coring technology requirements. The utilize the geotechnical majors for both coring and post-coring technology because the geotechnical majors' rarely offer to separate the two. The prestige of a geotechnical major also affords the client some liability protection in the event of catastrophy, such as an offshore platform failure.

There is presently no shortage of offshore geotechnical engineering expertise. However, there is not much choice in offshore geotechnical engineering companies. G-OCEAN's success in accomplishing the offshore 'hard part' - the downhole coring - will lead to further offshore geotechnical prominence.

THE BERLINERTOR

The OSA Survey-Drilling Vessel BERLINERTOR is not selected as the idea coring vessel, but rather as the available vessel. The vessel is presently not active in coring, while most contemporary coring vessels are active. UNDERSEA ASSOCIATES will detail a vessel/equipment inspection, operational history, modification recommendations and overall appraisal for the vessel in the G-OCEAN program.

In brief comparison with successful competitive US-flag coring vessels:

The BERLINERTOR has a high fixed derrick, which may contribute to vessel stability problems, and a heavy-class drilling system excessive to the vessel's water-depth mooring capacity. The US vessels use light-class FAILING 1500 drill rigs with folding derrick.

The BERLINERTOR uses 4½-inch drill pipe allowing 3-inch dia sampling and good opportunity for downhole techniques, such as in-situ vane and penetrometer. The US vessels use light 3½-inch upset flange drill pipe allowing 2-inch dia sampling, simple pipe handling and a drill string of approximately 1000-ft with the FAILING 1500 rig.

The BERLINERTOR has a bow thruster, a definite asset, and uses windlass and anchor chain for the bow moorings. The US vessels use drum winches and steel wire for all four moorings.

The BERLINERTOR is listed at 699 gross tonnage, and offers good personnel accomodations. The US vessels are constructed to be officially under 200 registered tonnage, to avoid greater crewing requirements, are are deficient in personnel accomudations.

(Berlinertor, cont.) p.7

The US vessels are supply vessels, with compromises in combining vessel, mooring system and drilling system, and are operated in routine coring performance at their maximum capability. The BERLINERTOR has compromises, but a performance potential greater than present capabilities

The offshore industry trend into deep water offers a profitable market for deep water/deep penetration coring. G-OCEAN's program is to commence operations with the BERLINERTOR competitive to contemporary successful coring vessels and progressively modify the vessel for superiority in deep water coring operations.

'Stage I' modifications may include replacement of the existing drilling system with a FAILING 1500 or 2500 system, or equivalent.

p.8

PERSONNEL

G-OCEAN will commence offshore operations with three key salaried personnel:

General Manager , with overall responsibility for the conduct of G-OCEAN, and reporting to the Board of Directors;

Administrative Secretary, with responsibility for office administration, accountability, communications, field logistical coordination, and marketing assistance;

Operations Manager , with responsibility for shipboard field operations and coordination with the vessel owners (CSA) and geotechnical participants (PM).

UNDERSEA ASSOCIATES will provide the principal marketing effort. However, marketing via high field performance and maintaining client goodwill will be tasked to all personnel from drilling roughnecks to the General Manager.

Potential key personnel resumes will be presented in the formal G-OCEAN proposal.

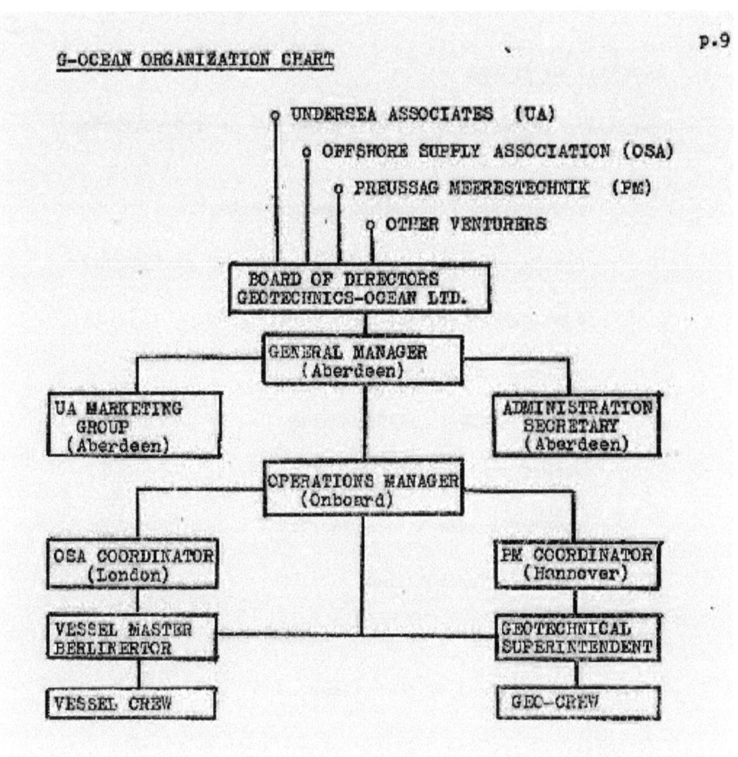

Demonstration of the BERLINATOR in book form is available on Google.

"**Notes on the Demonstration of the Drilling** Ship **'Berlinator'** ...*books.google.com/.../*_Notes on the Demonstration of the Drilling Ship 'Berlinator' 14-18 February, 1977: Institute of Geological Sciences, Marine Geology, Marine Geology Internal ..."

p.10

SCHEDULE OF EVENTS

G-OCEAN's formation will be implemented by the following schedule of events:

Preliminary Prospectus presentation.

Preliminary discussions by potential participants.

Preliminary Agreement to participate.

Relevant data acquisition.

Formal Proposal presentation.

Formal Agreement by participants.

G-OCEAN business incorporation.

Personnel recruiting.

Vessel outfitting and mobilization.

Commencement of operations.

Marketing of G-OCEAN services by UNDERSEA ASSOCIATES will be continuous throughout the Schedule of Events.

www.ingramcontent.com/pod-product-compliance
Ingram Content Group UK Ltd.
Pitfield, Milton Keynes, MK11 3LW, UK
UKHW041431210726
13854UKWH00010B/1656